You
Are a
Spiritual Being
Having a
Human Experience

You
Are a
Spiritual Being
Having a
Human Experience

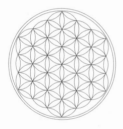

Bob Frissell

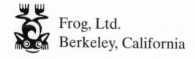

Frog, Ltd.
Berkeley, California

You Are a Spiritual Being Having a Human Experience

Published by Frog, Ltd.

Frog, Ltd. books are distributed by
North Atlantic Books
P.O. Box 12327
Berkeley, California 94712

ISBN 1-58394-033-2

Cover art by Spain Rodriguez
Cover and book design by Paula Morrison

Printed in the United States of America

1   2   3   4   5   6   7   8   9 / 05   04   03   02   01

Contents

Part IV: The Bible Code

Preface

Since the 1980s I have been a "Rebirther" by profession. I was trained by Leonard Orr in his now famous method for clearing emotional blockages and recovering the memory of one's birth, of one's pre-natal experiences, and beyond. I had been successfully conducting workshops in Rebirthing for many years, but in the late 1980s I became dissatisfied with my life as a Rebirther and the kind of service I was performing. Why were people coming to my workshops? Basically to solve their personal problems or to advance their careers; in short, to learn how to enhance their *material* well-being. Even when they were concerned with what they called their "relationships," their perspective on what this might mean was usually painfully materialistic and narrow. People did think about their "self-esteem," but what they meant was the state of their egos. Their highest aspirations were for a comfortable and pleasurable existence without irritating conflicts or anxieties; very few people felt concern for the welfare of others, or for what was really happening on the planet ecologically, or in the cosmos spiritually. The idealism of the '60s was dead and long-gone; methods for self-improvement were becoming more abundant and popular, and I was becoming quite tired of it. There was something terribly wrong with the way our culture was looking at life, and with the way I was coping with our culture. My own practice as a Rebirther had developed in a way that was personally very satisfying,

but just *that* seemed to be the problem. There had to be more
to existence than *personal* satisfaction. A piece of the puz-
zle was definitely missing.

All that changed dramatically early in the '90s when I discovered a whole new world of information that provided a
fresh perspective on what was happening not only in our society but on the Earth in general and, truly, in the universe as
a whole. Suddenly it all made sense again, and made sense
in a wonderful new way.

One of the things that began to bring things together for
me was my contact with Drunvalo Melchizedek, and I have
been presenting ideas and teaching workshops in the practices that have come to us through him since that time. I must
say that I continue to believe that these teachings are among
the researches and insights being presented on Earth today
that represent the greatest hope for the future of the planet.

Introduction

We are living at a time that is not only unique in human history—it is unique in the history of the entire universe—as far as anyone knows. We are accelerating in our evolution at such a rate that we have drawn the attention of beings from every part of the cosmos, because what happens to us will affect all life everywhere. And no one knows for sure what will happen to us.

The changes that are taking place are obvious to everyone even on our ordinary dimensional level. Technology is developing so rapidly that the scientists themselves cannot keep up with it. Knowledge in the form of new data about the universe is accumulating so fast from our radio telescopes and satellites and space probes that even NASA is already years behind in assimilating and integrating and interpreting it. At the same time because of ultra high-speed computers, theoreticians are able to generate theories at a rate so fast that there is no time or possibility of inventing experiments to test them!

Is this for the good or are we heading for disaster? Is there a pre-scripted scenario for our fate that has determined how it will all turn out? Or is it somehow up to us, or up to chance?

We know that our entire planet is being threatened by developments on what seems to be every level. The population continues to grow at a rate that makes it certain that very soon the Earth will not be able to sustain. Scientists in the European community are already predicting that within ten years there will not be enough fresh water for the population to drink. The efforts of countries like China to ensure that it will be able to feed its people are in themselves threatening the environment. Throughout the world, efforts to expand industrially so that "underdeveloped" peoples will be able to participate in the global economy are at the same time destroying local agriculture, causing vast disruption in local ways of life, and virtually enslaving local populations.

The world has become "one world" through electronic communications and ever more convenient jet transport, but the process itself is threatening the very existence of life on Earth.

At the same time predictions about enormous improvements in our life are almost as common as reasons for apprehensions of disaster. The genetic code has been deciphered and the entire genetic content of the human species, the "human genome," is all but completely understood. This, we are told, will bring enormous possibilities for curing and preventing cancer and other diseases. Advances in solar energy and other ways of tapping into the limitless supply of energy in the cosmos are just around the corner. The process of aging itself is close to being understood. We are told that within a decade human life expectancy may be a hundred and twenty years and that by the end of this century we will be virtually immortal. Yet for every advance there is a corresponding danger: the exploitation of bioengineering and biotechnology by selfish economic interests threatens to destroy our ability to sustain life in a natural way. Material technology seems to diminish our spiritual prowess. Every task that we teach machines to perform becomes a task we can no longer perform ourselves, throwing skilled workers out of work and turning time-honored skills into holdovers and relics.

At the same time changes in the condition of the Earth itself and in the solar system seem to be threatening life on Earth. Geologists know that both the axis of the Earth and the magnetic poles are due for a shift at any time. An enormous solar explosion on the sun in 1972 in fact would have destroyed all life on Earth if it had not been for the concern and intervention of the Sirians—beings from another stellar world who are intimately connected with our fate.

These historical and natural changes are just the external aspects of changes that are occurring in our very make-up as conscious beings. We are in the process of an accelerated spiritual evolution that is unprecedented in the known universe. Ancient prophecies and astrological theory together agree that we are living at a moment of great transition and change, but the rate of change that is occurring is something that has never been known before and was not anticipated by our most prescient sages.

The old world is dying and crying out to be saved; a new world is emerging and we are all being drawn into it. This new world offers incredible possibilities: a shift in the very nature of our consciousness and of the dimensional structure of the region of the world in which we live; a promise of "ascension" to a way of being where all the old conflicts melt away, and where harmony, love, and joy are the constant bases of our existence. But the passage to this new world seems fraught with struggle and disorientation. It doesn't seem that we are very well prepared to make this shift. Incompletions from our past—incomplete emotions, intentions, and personal histories lie dormant within us; and if they are not dealt with by each one of us, we will resist the coming changes. Resistance will cause us great suffering and prevent us from embracing the possibilities that are open to us.

The main message of this book is that we create reality itself unerringly and that the way we experience the changes that are occurring in us and about us depend entirely upon our own beliefs and most importantly on our own intention. We can resist change and create a context for our lives in which we are helpless victims, where we are at the effect of every seemingly external event that comes our way; or we can shift our identity through an awareness of the Unity of Being, and declare that we are spiritual masters with the power to create our own context of unity and harmony. Everything depends upon the purity of our intention—our ability to intend this shift of identity without hesitation and second thoughts, and get down to the business of integrating our incompletions from the past.

The basis for this shift in identity is not anything like a *fact* that can be demonstrated by external evidence; it is a *possibility* that you have to grasp intuitively: that we are right now and have been from the very beginning, a spiritual being who has chosen to be here on Earth at this time to be part of the process of the evolution of the planet. You may not be able to remember this choice, but, by reading this book and by working with the exercises that I have already presented in *Nothing in This Book Is True, But It's Exactly How Things Are,* and *Something in This Book Is True . . .* , you will be able to intuit what it means that *You Are a Spiritual Being Having a Human Experience.*

In this book, I want to present a picture of what the factors are in the transition that the planet and we as inhabitants of it are all going through, and how we are all very active players in what is happening. In a very real sense we are coming into a world that we ourselves are creating with our thoughts and our intentions. Though it is a universal law that we create our world with our consciousness, in the new conditions that are presently in formation, the immediacy of this connection between thought and reality will become incredibly clear. So will the intimacy of our connection with all life everywhere and our responsibility for creating the context for existence itself.

In the first part of the book I will expand and hopefully deepen the ideas behind some of the themes I struck in my other books: The dimensional structure of the cosmos, the Unity of Being, The nature of polarity. In the second section I want to go into the psychological and personal side of the evolution of consciousness: just how one's individual work—the release of incompletions from the past, the shift of identity from being a victim to being a spiritual master—are the keys not only to our own growth but to the evolution of the planet. In the third section, I will go into what we know and what we do not know about our present moment in the history of the planet, the galaxy, and Being itself. Particularly in this third section, I am not going to give definitive answers to all the questions I raise; but I will show how each of us can orient ourselves in these troublesome and exciting times—in spite of the fact that things have come to so unique a pass that not even the Ascended Masters and the Melchizedeks are positive about what is going on.

"It was the best of time and the worst of times," wrote Charles Dickens about the years of the French Revolution. It seems that there is a cosmic law at play, that where there is great hope there is also great danger: that where we seem on the brink of disaster, unimagined benefit may lie just around the corner.

PART I

The Unity
of Being

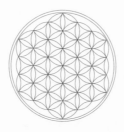

A World of Many Dimensions

The universe as a whole comprises an enormous numbers of levels or "dimensions" of being—each dimension possessing its own kind of reality and each being an expression of a different kind of consciousness. Dimensions overlap. We are living on the third dimension, but right now all the other dimensions of the planet Earth exist simultaneously interpenetrating each other, as if in the same place, each higher dimension including and adding a new perspective on the phenomena that appear on the ones below. The third dimension which we inhabit is the lowest level on which consciousness can take the form of intelligent, responsible life.

Now, our present-day human life is not only in the third dimension. We are also living on the *second level of consciousness*. I will explain the different levels of consciousness in a little while. But the second level of consciousness is a realm in which an awareness of the Unity of Being—the interconnectedness of all of life on all dimensions—is missing. We do not see it or know it or feel it, except at rare moments or in special states of consciousness. We perceive a world of separated things and beings. We perceive a *dualistic* world: a world that is divided—polarized—between things and events that appear to be good and those that appear to be evil. And we perceive a world that is thoroughly trapped in a kind of time in which things appear to exist for a while and then pass away into oblivion. I will have a lot more to say about the Unity of Being, the view that transcends duality, and about the nature of time as we go on.

Each dimension of being is organized energetically by a single wave-form—a single vibration that assembles and maintains the appearance of reality for all the beings who live on that dimension. In truth, that wave form is itself generated by those beings—it is the characteristic vibration of their mind-set and it gives the base-line sense of what they think is real. All we have to do to change our dimensional level is to change that base-line vibration, or, which amounts to the same thing, to become aware of other higher "frequencies"—the frequencies of the other dimensions.

The region of the universe to which we belong is organized like a musical scale: it comprises an "octave" in which the highest "note" repeats at a higher rate of vibration the basic characteristics of the lowest "note." Each note is a dimensional level. And just as the octave includes the twelve notes of the chromatic scale (on the piano all the white keys and the black keys together) plus a thirteenth note that is the first note of the next octave, so there are twelve main dimensional levels in our region of the universe. Now the musical scale actually includes more than these twelve main tones. There is a *continuum* of different "microtones" between any two notes. You can hear this on an instrument like a violin where a skillful player can "slide" continuously between the notes. In the Melchizedek's way of understanding the dimensional structure of our region of the universe, between each of the twelve main notes, there are an additional twelve specific "notes"; that is, twelve important dimensional levels, making 144 levels in all. The Melchizedeks call the additional levels just above or below a given dimension, the "overtones" of that dimension. (For those of you who are familiar with musical terminology, these should not be confused with the overtones or "partials" that go to make up the timbre or tone quality of the fundamental tones. But they are like these partials, since, like tone qualities, they do modify or "give color" to the twelve fundamental levels.)

The importance of this system of dimensional levels is that it provides a map of our own course of evolution. As we evolve as conscious beings, we ascend to higher and higher dimensional levels; that is, we achieve wider and wider perspectives on our own nature, each higher level encompassing the lower (as I mentioned); with each step we gain a deeper and wider sense of the Unity of Being, the One Spirit, that runs through them all.

The Five Levels of Awareness

When Atlantis fell, the dimensional level of the planet and its inhabitants fell from what must have been the higher overtones of the fourth dimension where the human species existed with Unity Consciousness, to the third dimension—the very bottom of the barrel as far as self-conscious life is concerned. But while we fell in dimensional level, this event itself was actually a necessary step in the progressive evolution of planetary consciousness. Here's why.

There are five levels of consciousness associated with life. These levels are not the same as the 144 dimensions and overtones of the octave. For instance, it is possible to exist on the higher overtones of the fourth dimension and be on the first level of consciousness. This was actually the case with the inhabitants of Atlantis and Lemuria. The higher overtones of the fourth dimension are also where we will be when we complete our own evolution to the next dimensional level. Where we are now, and where we have been for the past 13,000 years, is the second level. Where we are headed is the third level.

Now, the first, third, and fifth levels involve different degrees of awareness of the Unity of Being and are fundamentally in harmony with it, while the second and fourth levels are "disharmonic." On the second and fourth levels there is no awareness of Unity. The consequence is that on those levels life shows all kinds of conflicts and other inharmonious and dysfunctional phenomena. The second and fourth levels, however, are necessary as stepping stones in order to evolve from the first to the third or from the third to the fifth levels.

The first level, in other words, in evolutionary terms, is a more primitive mode of consciousness than our own, even though people on that level experienced a form of Unity Consciousness and we do not, and even though the Atlantean world was a world in the fourth dimension. On the third level, we will experience Unity Consciousness of a higher, more fully evolved form. There is a very neat and clear explanation of just why these levels have the properties they do, which I present in my Flower of Life workshops. It is based on Sacred Geometry and the logic that lies behind it.

The important point for our purposes is that the inhabitants of Atlantis were on the first level. Where we are now is the second level. And where we are going is the third level.

The beings on the three levels are differentiated by physical height, by the number of chromosomes the genetic material in the cells are made up of, and in the kind of memory that they have, i.e., in the way that they have access to the past. For instance, the height range on the first level was three to five feet, while on the third level it will be ten to sixteen feet. I went into the exact differences in chromosome numbers in *Nothing,* and if you are interested you can find out the details there. The type of memory available on the first level is called Dream Time Memory. The present day Australian Aborigines (who never mutated from the first level to the second, perhaps because they never developed writing) know of a mode of being that the they call *"Alcheringa,"* which in fact means "The Dream Time," and from their point of view The Dream Time is the very basis of reality. Fundamentally, in Dream-Time Memory, people are able to recreate anything that has happened in the past holographically. For example, if a tribal meeting were held yesterday, and if an Aboriginal had been present at that meeting, he or she could recreate the entire scene holographically, including everything that was said and everything that was done. Pretty much like the "holodeck" in Star Trek. If someone else were to step into the recreated scene they would be able to relive every moment of it.

On the third level of consciousness we will have what is called "Real Time" memory. With Real-Time Memory whatever you think is real manifests as such immediately: reality is instantaneously a function or a product of a thought or a feeling. You think it, and bingo! it appears as a real thing in front of you. If you think of yesterday's meeting, you won't be recreating a holographic replica of it, you will actually *be* there. Past and present and future are all available in this way, because in a sense they are all happening at once: time itself is not a straight line, as it seems to be on our second level, but is more like a sphere. So this kind of access to the past is part of a higher level of consciousness as compared to the Dream Time of the first level. The first level with its Dream Time is a form of Unity Consciousness, but a lower from than the third level. It is possible to be on one of the higher overtones of the fourth dimension where Unity Consciousness manifests as the Dream Time of the first level of consciousness.

On the second level of consciousness we have to rely on our rather weak personal memories and the various technical aids we have invented to enhance it. As a matter of fact, it was the invention of writing itself that clinched the passage from the first to the second level, from the passage from

Dream-Time Memory, to the weak memories of our present level of consciousness. Apparently, traces of Dream Time survived well into the present era. During the very early days of the civilization of Egypt—about 5000 years ago—an Ascended Master who was known in Egypt as the god Thoth introduced writing for the very purpose of once and for all throwing the human race out of the Dream Time.

The Melchizedeks

Drunvalo's second name is the name for a special class of beings who have attained the ability to move freely throughout the 144 different worlds or dimensions of reality that make up our "octave"—our region of the universe. They have encompassed all the levels. They know the whole scale. All the different perspectives, all the different modes of consciousness, are freely available to them. They can tune in to the different vibrational levels at will. When a person becomes a Melchizedek, he or she is faced with a choice. They can leave this part of the universe altogether and enter into a thirteenth dimension—a dimension that exists outside the octave. It is a new world where *everything* is different. In contrast to this, when we pass from one dimension of reality to another dimension *within* the octave, that is, within this part of the universe—when we pass, say, from the third to the fourth dimension—things will be different in many respects, but there will be a basic connection that links the different levels. Each higher level will be a wider view of the ones below. But when you leave the octave, nothing whatsoever is the same. You enter a whole new space. To do so is to begin a whole new phase of existence, to enter upon an entirely new phase of one's evolution. But the Melchizedek does not necessarily leave the octave. There is another choice: to remain in this octave and serve as a troubleshooter for problems that arise here—problems affecting life as a whole, or the interrelationships between the different levels, or problems that arise between this region of the universe and the universe as a whole. A Melchizedek who makes this choice is a bit like what the Buddhist's call a *"bodhisattva"*—a being who has foregone the possibility of entering into nirvana—of becoming a buddha—for the sake of assisting other sentient beings. Drunvalo long ago made this decision. At the present he is on an assignment in our world that is intimately connected with helping our planet pass harmoniously on to the next stage of its own evolution.

In order to fulfill his mission it was necessary for Drunvalo to take the form of an ordinary mature human being and to live his life among us without the appearance of being a magical or supernatural entity. It was necessary that he really be an ordinary person in order to communicate most successfully with as many of us as possible. If you have the opportunity to take a workshop with him or to see his video tapes or hear him speak, I am sure you will agree that there doesn't seem to be anything very out of the ordinary about him at all. As a matter of fact, he actually is an ordinary human being at the same time that he is a Melchizedek. This is because Drunvalo is what we call a "walk-in." A walk-in is a being from a higher dimensional reality who has made a benevolent arrangement with an ordinary human being so that he can occupy a human body and personality in order to fulfill his task. Drunvalo "walked in" in April of 1972. The person whose body he now occupies agreed to pass on, in exchange for which his spiritual evolution was sped up and enhanced.

Drunvalo says that when he first entered his host's body he could remember most of what his actual identity and life had been. But shortly thereafter, the vividness of these memories faded, and so today, though he has access to higher dimensional realities in meditation and by other means, by and large he is pretty much like any other human being. The truth is, however, that *he is a higher dimensional being having a human experience*—and he knows it. And the essence of what I have to say here is that *we are all spiritual beings— higher dimensional beings—having a human experience*— an experience on the third dimensional level—but we have for very specific reasons having to do with the history of this planet—forgotten this basic truth.

Thoth

Drunvalo's work was greatly assisted by his fellowship with Thoth, an Ascended Master who had been on Earth for literally thousands and thousands of years. An Ascended Master is, in the total scheme of things, on a lower level than a Melchizedek. A Melchizedek is a master of the entire octave, while an Ascended Master has a more limited ability: he can regenerate his physical body at will and pass to another body without losing his memory. But since Drunvalo had lost much of his memory when he assumed his current human form, his association with Thoth proved extremely useful. Thoth was able to keep Drunvalo informed on many subjects relevant to Drunvalo's mission that he would not have otherwise been aware of. Drunvalo did have access to two angelic beings as instructors and guides, but they have not been available on a regular, human-to-human basis. Since Thoth himself had been intimately involved in many stages of the history of the Earth, he was well-prepared to be Drunvalo's companion-in-arms as it were.

Thoth had lived in Atlantis as a member of a family that already had known the principle of physical immortality for more than a hundred thousand years. He was in fact the King of Atlantis, with the name of Chiquetet Arlich Vomalites. After the fall of Atlantis he, together with other Ascended

Masters, initiated the reconstruction of the new grid of Unity Consciousness that today is part of the picture of the next phase in terrestrial evolution.

With the rise of Egyptian civilization he took the identity of the Egyptian deity, Thoth, as I mentioned before. He was the god associated with magic—a sort of shape-shifter, taking on innumerable forms. It was part of his nature to change his nature. He was said to be the "intelligence" that accompanied the other gods—it was not that he had ideas or opinions of his own. He stimulated them in others. He was the god of the intellect par excellence. and it was Thoth that brought writing to the Egyptians in order to complete the process of the human race's passage from the first to the second level of consciousness.

After the decline of Egyptian civilization Thoth became known as the Greek god Hermes. In Greece he was the messenger of the gods, but what that really meant was pretty much the same thing as the god Thoth signified in Egypt. He was a go-between—his provenance was the principle of communication—the spirit that allowed information to pass between gods and gods or gods and humans.

Hermes was known as a god that dwelled at cross-roads, places far from cities at intersections where people from different countries would pass on their travels. He was an inhabitor of no-mans lands, of places between things. Wherever and whenever things were changing into other things, wherever there was a gap in the identity of things: the gap between the underworld and the Earth or between life and death, for instance—there you would find Hermes. Hermes was also a great teacher and an initiator into mysteries, since initiation always and everywhere involves the transition between one state of being and another.

One of his most important initiates was the Greek philosopher Pythagoras, known to every high school student as the

originator of the "Pythagorean Theorem" about sides and
hypotenuses of triangles. Pythagoras was a friend and student of Hermes/Thoth, and his practice of geometry was actually part of his teaching of Sacred Geometry, which, of course,
he learned from Thoth. The basis of Western music, archi-
tecture and the fine arts has its roots in Pythagoras' school,
and so there is a direct connection between much of high
Western Culture and Thoth's personal intervention.

Thoth has remained alive throughout the entire history
of the West until very recently—actually until May 4, 1991.
From November 1, 1984 until Thoth's departure, Thoth was
in direct contact with Drunvalo, and it is partly through this
contact that Drunvalo, as I mentioned, was able to maintain
much of his knowledge, in spite of the fact that his memory
of his own state had decayed. (The other way that Drunvalo
maintained contact with his own higher knowledge was through
access to a pair of angelic beings who contact him periodi-
cally and whom he is able to contact when necessary.)

The Ascended Masters Ascend

Thoth mentioned to Drunvalo before he left in 1991, how
the Ascended Masters had thought that the planet was going
to rise collectively into the fourth dimension the previous
year because of certain things that were coming to a head
during the time of what turned out to be "Desert Storm"—
the Gulf War. During the last weeks of August in 1990 they
thought that the planet would reach a certain "critical mass"
in terms of the various factors necessary for Ascension to
occur. Then from Jan. 10th to 19th, 1991 the energies of the
terrestrial plane would come to a focus.

January 10th to 19th is a very special time period, hyper-
dimensionally. A kind of "time vault" opens up in the Great
Pyramid in Egypt, and if you know how to use it, an opening

to hyper-dimensional reality becomes available. Drunvalo had gone to Egypt during that period on two other occasions, under Thoth's instructions, for special initiations. They felt that during the week of January 10 to 19, 1991 some major world-wide event would bring the world, or much of the world, into unity, and that by the spring of that year, we would all ascend collectively into the new dimensional level. The Ascended Masters themselves would act as a catalyst to help us along. They had planned to take off in a single group and ascend as far out dimensionally as they could, thinking that their own ascension would act as a trigger to pull the planet up. They anticipated that if they succeeded it would have been a pretty rough ride for the inhabitants of Earth—the culmination of various catastrophes and disasters foretold in various prophecies—but in the end we would all land in a completely transformed world. But during the critical period, exactly in that time window, we physically attacked Iraq. That was January 15, 1991. The Ascended Masters were looking for the Earth to come together in some form of unity. Well we came together, alright: essentially the entire world organized against Saddam Hussein, but I don't think that's the kind of unity they were looking for, and so the masters held off and did not attempt the Ascension.

Something did, however, occur between January to May of that year, although we don't exactly what. On May 4, Thoth came to Drunvalo and said that their work together was complete. But he reiterated something that he had already hinted at—that things were starting to look a "little weird"—that things were happening on Earth that the Ascended Masters could not completely account for, having to do with the rapid acceleration of planetary evolution due to the Sirian intervention and the holographic protection field the Sirians had created to keep Earth from being absorbed into the sun. Thoth told Drunvalo that our situation didn't look like what they thought it would, but that on May 4 they were going to leave anyway. He said that they'd figured out how to get into the next octave, and that they'd come up with a new plan. Rather than all the Masters ascending at once and propelling the planet up that way, they now were going to take off in groups of 32 in a group Merkaba that was designed to take them over the "Great Wall"—the barrier between the octaves— and into the 13th dimension.

He gave Drunvalo that information—how they'd figured out how to get into the next octave—and on that day, Thoth along with his wife Shesat and thirty other Ascended Masters took off.

The formation of the group Merkaba, Drunvalo says, in fact did work. And this is another factor that should cause us to anticipate that planetary Ascension is a reality. Before Thoth left he instructed Drunvalo to give a certain workshop, called the "Tri-Phase Workshop." This involved giving instructions in the formation of the group Merkaba like the one the Ascended Masters had departed in. At first Drunvalo couldn't understand why he was being given instructions to give this workshop, because it didn't seem like we were remotely close to being ready to form such groups and Ascend. But it turned out that the purpose of the instructions was not to teach human beings, so much as to wake up the planet, to wake up Mother Earth and *her* Merkaba field, which had been literally dormant for 13,000 years. And so, if that's true, Earth's Merkaba field is now active again.

Creating Reality

I am telling all of this at this point to give you a *context* for the rest of what I am going to be imparting to you. When I say that we are spiritual beings, I mean that we are involved in matters of very broad and general concern. Our spiritual work is not just about our own personal happiness. It is about the fate of the planet and actually more than that—the fate of all life everywhere. We have taken human form in order help the birthing of the planet onto the next dimensional level. And in order to achieve our own "ascension" we need to identify ourselves with this fact and this task.

Now what does it mean that we are spiritual beings having a human experience?

What is it specifically that spiritual beings are and do and just what is this "human experience" that we are in the midst of?

The basic idea is that, as spiritual beings, it is our business to *create reality*. It is also our business to create what is *not* reality. I mean, if we live in ignorance and illusion, this is just as much our creation as is living in awareness and truth. And this is the case whether we know it or not, whether we *like* it or not, whether we *understand* it or not. It doesn't matter. Reality is our creation, 100% of the time, whether we acknowledge the fact or whether we are ignorant of it or whether we deny it. The only distinction is that if we know it and acknowledge it, we have the opportunity to create reality consciously. And if we don't know it, or if we know it and don't like it or some variation thereof, we *still* create reality, but we do it unconsciously or in a way that puts us at the effect of life, so that we become victims having no power.

Reality itself is therefore a function of our consciousness. And that means that whenever we are facing problems or difficulties, whatever the problem might be, whether it is a personal problem, or a global or universal problem, it can only be solved by consciousness. So if it's true that we create reality unerringly 100% of the time without exception; and if we acknowledge this; and if we simply assert that that is true—we become, potentially, extremely powerful. We *are* extremely powerful. Yet the sorry truth is that most of us, most of the time, look at ourselves as though we had no power. And that is the "human" part of the formula: "we are spiritual beings having a human experience." The human being has forgotten his or her power. Essentially and for the most part we do not recognize that we are the creators of our own reality, so when we experience difficulties and problems of any kind, we feel ourselves to be victims, at the mercy of circumstances, the whim of the gods, the bearers of "bad karma," unworthy of success or happiness—you name it. Though as spiritual beings we are the *authors* of our circumstances and the ultimate *authorities* on how and why things are the way they are, as human beings we think we have no responsibility for our own suffering—though we are quick to take the credit for things when they turn out well, (usually blindly and without understanding in what sense the credit really does belong to us).

So the first corollary to acknowledging that we create reality by our consciousness is that we have responsibility for the reality we create, that we are the authors of and authorities on our own existence and our own world. If you are willing to stand up and say "it's time to wake up," you have to take responsibility for the whole process and you have to begin to deal with things that previously slipped under the table. You have to look at things in your personal life that previously, perhaps, you were not looking at, and you have to recognize that the more general conditions of life on Earth— what is happening to this planet and what is happening to other people and what is happening to human society—is your responsibility too. So we have tremendous power— potential power for the most part—but real power nevertheless. And responsibility and power go hand-in-hand. It's a matter of the ability to step up to the plate and using our opportunity wisely, using it responsibly, and using it in a way that is for the greatest good of all concerned. And what I mean by "all concerned" is all life everywhere. And not only all of life, but all of Being itself.

Victim Mentality

Being a spiritual being having a human experience is inconsistent with what you might call a "victim mentality"—the mindset wherein we take no responsibility for who we are—for how powerful our thoughts and our feelings and our actions are.

The victim mentality is nothing new. It isn't something that just began to come over us yesterday, or that emerged with the modern world. It is not, as many people believe today, the result of our loss of belief in traditional religion, or our liberal political ideas, or the decay of family values or anything like that. The victim mentality has actually been with us for roughly 13,000 years, since the poles shifted, the continent of Atlantis fell into the sea, and the consciousness of the human race passed from the first to the second level. A basic characteristic of the second level of consciousness is a sense of separation between ourselves and the rest of Being. We look at ourselves as apart from other beings, and when we experience something unpleasant, we think that these other beings have "caused" it. In other words: we think we are victims. This sense of separation also makes us believe that what we think and what we feel and what we do have no real impact on what is outside of ourselves; that we are not responsible for our lives or for the condition of our planet; that our thoughts are our private concerns, and since nobody knows what we are thinking or feeling inside, what does it matter anyway? It's not true. We create reality unerringly. Period. What you think matters. It and nothing else creates the world. You are the author and the authority for your being, and for Being itself.

Reclaiming Your Authority

For the last 13,000 years, as I say, we have been giving our power away; and one of the ways we have been doing that is by thinking that *authority* lies outside of us. Authority in what sense? Authority in every sense: authority for judging what we ought to do and ought not to do, authority for deciding what is real and what is not real.

In our present day world, the way we most typically give away our authority is by believing that every area of life is only understood by "experts," people who specialize in some form of knowledge and therefore really know more than we could possibly know about it. We have experts in health and experts in finance and experts in plumbing and experts in how to groom the dog. The average "well-adjusted" human won't make a move without *consulting* someone whom he thinks knows more than he does. This expert-trusting mentality is enormously reinforced by the success of left-brain technology: the ability to predict and control the occurrence of material phenomena by what amounts to little more than very sophisticated cunning and stealth! Having forgotten that we ourselves create the reality we want to control, we think we need to do it by a subterfuge, deftly manipulating nature as if behind nature's back. But the truth is that the enormously impressive feats of contemporary technology; the details of which indeed lie far beyond the knowledge and capabilities of most of us; have the effect of making us feel powerless and ignorant in spite of the incredible things they empower us to do and the incredible knowledge on which they are based. There is a very crazy paradox, a contradiction, here: that things that should empower us in fact cripple us; that knowledge increases our feeling of ignorance;

that the ability to manipulate and control nature only rein-
forces our completely false belief that nature is something
other than ourselves, something that we are from the beginning *not* in control of, and thus have to conquer or dominate
or manage. And when we fail to manage it—when we get
sick or find the planet on the brink of ecological catastrophe—we think the only way out of the mess is more technology. More expert monkey business. More giving away of
our power.

The truth is that the technological "progress" of humanity has proven disastrous in many ways. The steps we take to
control the environment or improve our health by material,
technological means very often create unforeseen side-effects
that make problems for us that are greater than the ones we
set out to solve. People die in hospitals every day from diseases that they contracted there, or from the deterioration of
their physical bodies brought about through medications and
violent therapeutic interventions. And when we use external
technology to achieve desired results, we neglect to search
within ourselves for *internal* means that might achieve the
same ends. There are no technologically producible effects
that we could not achieve without technological aid, if we
were only aware of our full potential. Every gain in external
technology is thus a loss in internal power. When we first
learned to write—this happened for most of the human race
when Thoth introduced writing to the Egyptians and the
Sumerians, as I mentioned before, there was an enormous
loss in our ability to use our memory. With rapid transporta-
tion systems we have gradually lost our ability to run and walk
long distances. We have developed technologically enhanced
agricultural processes, creating a food-production industry
organized as big business, and have completely lost the ability to produce our own food and sustain our families and communities without relying on multi-national food conglomerates

and the entire global economy. In every instance, by depending on technological, left-brained approaches to enhancing
our existence, we have abandoned our inner potential—we
have given away our power.

When Drunvalo realized what was going on, at first he
thought he needed to reject all technology to accomplish his
mission. But after several years of working this way, his angels
appeared to him and gave him a little bit of a course-cor-
rection. They let him know that it is not technology *per se*
that is the problem; it is the kind of technology we are developing and the whole mental frame we have adopted to do
so. We do not need to reject technology; we need to discover
an *internal* technology, a technology that includes the work
of the emotional and intuitive right hemisphere of our brain
to complement the intellectually dominated left-brain technology that we have today. And the basis of this right-brain
technology is the recognition that the reality we wish to *change,*
is in fact a reality that we *create*. We've been going at it the
wrong way around.

Another way that we fail to recognize our own authority,
our own *authorship* of our world, is by surrendering the right
to evaluate and judge our own activities to our governmen-
tal authorities, religious teachers, and to attitudes that are
created for us by the media. We believe that how we should
behave and what we ought to think and feel can be determined by rules and interests and images that lie outside of
ourselves. We let radio preachers or TV news commentators
form our minds. We let advertising images manipulate our
attitudes and direct our desires. No one wants to admit that
this is so, yet the billions of advertising dollars spent annu-
ally say that it is. Advertising not only sells products: it sells
the images that are connected to the products and the images
of the life styles that make it desirable to have what the com-
mercial wants you to buy. There is a kind of secret logic at

work here: you see an image which you half-consciously think is *you*, someone like you, or someone you feel you *ought* to be like. And that person is driving a certain vehicle or drinking a certain kind of beer, and *therefore*, to be yourself, i.e., to be *like* the person with whose image you identify, you have to drive or drink one too. There is no limit to the images that are offered, no limit to the number of ways we might be attracted to thinking that we are. There are images for everyone. A real democracy of images. And each image is manipulated cynically to make you buy some product or some service, and every time you half-consciously identify with anyone of these images, no matter what it is, you are giving away your authority, your ability to freely determine your own reality, your own way of being.

We live in a world in which we seem to be constantly asked to surrender our center, to give up our authority over what we believe to be real and true and over what we believe we should be and do. This process of surrendering does actually correspond to the reality, not of our ultimate nature, but of the dimensional level that we are living on. In order to be taken in by an image presented in an ad campaign, it must be the case that we are living on a level where we are susceptible to such manipulation. We must actually profoundly doubt our own independent ability to decide for ourselves what is right and wrong, what is desirable or not, or what is true and false. We ask ourselves who are we to determine such things? We don't have a strong sense of who we are, so we wish to become what we see. We wish to become whatever image appeals to what we feel we lack.

All of this has implications for our relation to spiritual reality. If we for a moment imagine that the spirit is real, we think that it must be fundamentally different from our very selves; it must be something that does not have to do with the center of our being; it must be like an image, so we try to

conform to some image of what we think a spiritual person
might be. This image doesn't have to come from TV ads. We
pick it up most commonly through conventional religious
teachings. If we are brought up in a conventional religious
context, or even if we have just absorbed by a kind osmosis
the general ideas that are available about religion in our culture, we may believe that, if we play by the rules, respect
"authority," and believe in God, perhaps, after we die, we
will be rewarded for all our sufferings and struggles, and all
the injustice that we see in life will be set right. At rare moments we may catch a glimpse of something beyond. We may
be inspired to a belief in "spiritual reality," and a sense that
there is more to existence than the physical world and its
obvious limitations. But somehow we think that this spiritual
reality, just like material reality, is something outside of our
core, something that is added onto the world, or beyond the
world, or that it is some kind of magical presence that mys-
teriously shows up here or there, who knows why, to defy the
"laws of nature" and produce miracles. And if we actually
witness one of these so-called miracles, if we experience some
extraordinary phenomenon; if a dream we have comes true,
or if we have a vision or a momentary sense of meaningful
elation in communing with nature or contemplating art or in
a state of meditation, we feel that we are still mere, ordinary
human beings; only now we are having a "spiritual" experience. It isn't so. We are spiritual beings from the get go!

So the distinction that I'm getting at is that because of the
reality we have unwittingly created for ourselves, where we
see ourselves as powerless victims of forces beyond our control and with no authority over our lives, we have no access
to our spiritual essence, and therefore we have no access to
our true potential. And when we do per chance catch a glimpse
of our true nature, when we do occasionally have a spiritual
experience, we tend to view ourselves as not being good

enough and not being up to the task. We may wish to go further into this business of spiritual reality, even to the point of reading books and taking workshops and trying out all sorts of different methods of self-improvement; but when it comes right down to actually stepping into what these teachings are all about, we don't really dare. And I think that a lot of people come to what you might call the self-improvement movement, "New-Age Spirituality," or whatever other names it has, thinking along such lines. We buy all the books, attend workshop after workshop, thinking that true understanding is just around the corner, hoping that being in the presence of the latest guru or mastering the latest meditation technique or going on the latest "trip" will magically make us good enough so that finally we'll begin to understand. But the truth is there's nothing to understand that is not in our very nature from the beginning. The only trip worth taking is the one that leads you to where you already are.

Sacred Geometry

It is all well and good if I tell you that you yourself are already a spiritual being. The problem is how can you know this and feel this, not because I say it is so, but because you know it is so from your very being. Now everything that the mind knows and everything that your heart feels, is a form of *Being*, and so if I can help you understand Being and feel its meaning, I will have gone a long way in accomplishing this task. And what I have to say is first of all that Being is a perfect unity, and that you yourself are not only *a* being—but that at root you are Being itself! This will take some explaining.

In my first book, *Nothing in This Books is True—But It's Exactly How Things Are,* I spent a lot of words explaining what I learned from Drunvalo about Sacred Geometry. The point of that was to show that everything—and I do mean

everything, underline it—everything without exception can
be shown to come to us through a single image. And here I
am not talking about an external image—the image of life
styles like the ones depicted in the media that I was talking
about a moment ago—but an inner image: a *structure* that
forms what we are from within, and that can be symbolized
through an image that we can see. In *Nothing* I used the language of Sacred Geometry to demonstrate this image, this
structure. Physicists or mathematicians tell us that number
is the structure behind all reality, but what seems more true
is that it is rather *shape* and the laws of shape that Sacred
Geometry spells out. And that includes ourselves—our minds
and our bodies. Everything visible can be derived from a single geometrical form. The idea was that if we could see that
everything including ourselves comes from this image, our
minds would be able to grasp and our hearts feel the Unity
of Being and our own identity with it. On the second level
of consciousness, we do not see this unity and we do not feel
this identity. We see separation, division, distinction at every
point. We create a reality in which unity is something very
remote, almost incomprehensible. We hardly understand
what the Unity of Being is, let alone that we ourselves are
not only expressions of it, but in our very essence this unity
itself. So I want to look a little more closely now at what the
Unity of Being really means, what it is that Sacred Geometry and the Flower of Life symbolize.

The Unity of Being

What do I mean by the Unity of Being? First of all I mean that
all existence—everything that exists in any way, everything
that exists on every dimension—is part of a single, integral
whole. One comprehensive Reality. Everything that has ever
been seen or felt or experienced or dreamed or imagined by a

human being or by any type of being whatsoever—belongs to it. Nothing is left out. Even purely unreal or imaginary things exist *as* imagined. In a way it's obvious: everything that exists or ever existed or ever will exist—*exists!* It sounds almost silly or trivial or, to use a term from logic, *tautological.* But it has a profound implication; it isn't silly or trivial at all. It means that there is nothing whatsoever that is excluded from Being. There is no such thing as a "Non-Being." There are no "non-entities." There is no possibility of ultimate separation, no possibility of being ultimately cast off or lost or left out of the totality of Being.

We will see that in fact it has an even more extraordinary implication than that, for the ultimate meaning of the Unity of Being is that we ourselves, each one of us, just as we already actually are, is Being itself. This may sound a bit astounding. And in fact it *is* astounding! It is the deepest mystery and most astounding truth in the whole of—Being! But the ultimate promise of all the great world religions, and the hopes of our own modern scientific culture as well, are no less astounding. I mean the ideas of the immortality of the soul in Western religions, of the possibility of spiritual liberation in Asian faiths, and the mastery of physical nature in modern science. But the ultimate possibility for all of these things must come from what is ultimately true, from the truth of Being itself, for nothing is possible except what in a sense is inscribed in the ultimate nature of reality. And the ultimate nature of reality is Being itself.

Now as a matter of fact the Unity of Being has been, in a rather veiled way, a major theme, in slightly different forms, in all the major world religions. It is also true that each religion has a more or less secret tradition in which the goal of religious observance is to seek *union* with God or with ultimate reality. This view has often been kept secret because it is both difficult to understand and very easy to abuse. For if

I achieve oneness with the source of everything, conventional religion with its authoritarian attitude, its churches and priests and gurus and other leaders, cannot have any power over me. I discover in myself the authority for my own existence. But in spite of this threat to their authority, even conventional religions have proclaimed the Unity of Being, albeit in an obscure way.

Unity in Conventional Religion

Each of the three great Western religious traditions proclaim a faith in the One God. Each has its own fundamental proclamation about that belief, and each one is a proclamation of Unity. The most holy and revered utterance in Judaism, the "Shmah," announces: "Hear Oh Israel, The Lord God—the Lord is One." The unpronounceable Hebrew name for God, YHVH, actually means the One Who IS, Who Was, and Who Will Be. YHVH is Being. Therefore: Being is One. The Moslems epitomize their faith in Allah with the motto, "There is no god but God." And the first article in the Nicean Creed of Christianity is "Credo in Unam Deum," "I believe in One God."

The Eastern faiths, Hinduism, Buddhism, Taoism, which do not tend to symbolize the Unity of Being in a personal God, are each in its own way based on a principle of oneness nevertheless. In Hinduism, the world is full of innumerable deities, bound together through an incredibly complex web of myths and legends and family and tribal relationships. But all those gods and heroes as well as all human beings and animals, are understood to be reflections of "Brahm," the one great ocean of Existence, Consciousness, and Bliss. And in Buddhism, though all beings are considered to be "empty" or devoid of an ultimate self, that *emptiness* is not *nothingness*. It expresses the deep truth that all apparently separate and singular things are completely interrelated and dependent for their very existence not only on each other but on the whole fabric of reality. Even for the Buddhist, all Being is one.

For the Chinese Taoists, the one reality is envisioned as The Great Tao, the vast path or roadway that conducts all things according to their inner nature, dividing into two always complementary and interdependent tendencies, the Yin and the Yang. The manifest world occurs in pairs of opposites—dark and light, aggressive and yielding, active and passive—but these pairs always function together in unity. Finally, tribal societies the world over each in its own way holds beliefs that show a feeling for unity: the Great Spirit of the Native Americans, or the world of the Dream Time of the Aboriginal Australians.

Unity in Greece and Egypt

Perhaps the most comprehensive and radical vision of the Unity of Being was the view of the ancient Greek healer, law giver, poet, visionary, and philosopher, Parmenides of Elea. Parmenides taught that not only is all reality One, but that nothing except Being itself truly IS at all. Everything "else," is mere appearance, yet there is always a connection between what merely appears and what truly is, because everything that appears, appears to *be*. (There is plenty more to say about this saying, "that everything that appears, appears to be." It is the key to how things can appear to be separate entities and yet in fact be One.) All that we think of as existing—material objects, persons, thoughts, or gods—are expressions of Being itself, and at bottom are nothing *but* Being itself.

Before Parmenides (who lived in the 6th century B.C.) other Greek thinkers also attempted to arrive at a concept of the Unity of Being, one thinker asserting that everything is like water, another that everything is like earth, a third that everything is flux or change, another that everything is number. But Parmenides seems to have made the ultimate discovery: that reality is not unified through being *like* any of these things, but through the fact of Being itself.

Actually, all these attempts by religions and philosophers to express the Unity of Being owe their insight to a dim recollection of the doctrine taught by the great heretical Egyptian Pharaoh, Akhunaton. Akhunaton came to Egypt in 1355 B.C. and in a period of $17\frac{1}{2}$ years introduced a completely new concept to the Egyptians, who up until that time (and in fact, after Akhunaton's brief reign) believed in many gods, many diverse types of reality. It was he who introduced the idea that there was only one god, that Being was ultimately unity. Akhunaton came to Egypt on a mission. He was in fact a Sirian. He came from the companion star to Sirius as part of the cosmic plan to reintroduce the higher level of consciousness that had been lost to the inhabitants of this planet since the fall of Atlantis, more than 10,000 years before, and to accelerate the process of restoring the damaged grid of energy surrounding and permeating the Earth. The hallmark of this higher level of consciousness was in fact awareness of the Unity of Being, and the sole purpose of the Mystery School that Akhunaton created, was to reintroduce the concept of the Unity of Being, to re-seed the planet, as it were, with this vision of truth, and ultimately lead the Earth to the next level of consciousness. His specific mission was to put back the idea of the Unity of Being into the Akashic Record, and he used the sun as a symbol of that unity. He knew that after his rule it would be forgotten, but it didn't matter. The idea, and therefore the *possibility,* of the Unity of Being had been restored.

Now one of the things that is really striking about Parmenides is that he taught that Being itself is like a vast and luminous "well-rounded sphere," indivisible, without internal difference or blemish, eternal, timeless, whole. It had no beginning, for how could Being itself have started at one time rather than at another, since it contained *all* time and was itself utterly timeless? And in it there could be no distinct past or future, since it is all *now*. This image of a perfect sphere, incidentally, appears in most of the great religions that I mentioned as a very pure vision and symbol of the one reality. And this idea of a perfect, timeless, ultimate reality has always remained poised, lofty, remote, breathtakingly grand and beautiful beyond, the conflicts and differences of ordinary apparent existence. "The One remains, The Many change and Pass / ... Life like a dome of many colored glass/ Stains the white radiance of eternity," writes Shelley, the English Romantic poet.

Now the ancient Greeks in their deepest traditions, always considered themselves the heirs and students of the ancient Egyptians. And they felt this most particularly regarding their own traditions of Sacred Geometry, which they used to build their temples, to bestow serenity and a sense of eternal balance on their art, and to provide an ideal for their most elevated thought. And ultimately, all of Sacred Geometry can be understood as a meditation on the Unity of Being through the analysis of the great symbolic sphere.

The Many and the One: The Merkaba

According to the Melchizedeks, the Unity of Being is expressed specifically through a figure of Sacred Geometry known as The Flower of Life, and this figure is itself based on the sphere. The Unity of Being is expressed in each one of us through the existence of a protective energy field encompassing and surrounding our physical body called the

Figure 1–1. A star tetrahedron.

Merkaba. The Merkaba is based on a star tetrahedron inscribed in a sphere *(figure 1.1)*, and this in turn is derived
from the Flower of Life *(figure 1.2)*. How its structure relates
to Sacred Geometry is described in *Nothing*. In fact everything has its Merkaba, its space-time-energy vehicle, that is
the deep link it has with the Unity of Being. The Merkaba
acts as a kind of go-between, connecting the individual
appearance of things with the fact that in their innermost
reality they are Being itself.

   The world itself, on every dimensional level, is made, as
Parmenides says, of things "that appear to be": trees and
stones and turtles and automobiles and planets and oceans
and thoughts and microbes and bones and restaurants and

continents and nation states and multinational corporations and "the secret government" and you and me. Each thing appears to have its own separate existence, its boundary or outline that separates it from every other thing and makes it be itself. But it is only itself by being distinct from all the others. Even in its separation from others, it is dependent on others, dependent on the system of differences that makes up the whole. Yet as an individual, it expresses the principle of unity and individuality that belongs to that whole. Every apparent thing is therefore a "one," both in that it is *apparently* distinct from all the others, and in that it truly reflects the one reality. In the very fact of its appearing to exist as a single thing, it reflects and expresses the Unity of Being. There is an old saying, "The One produces a One." The Unity of Being expresses itself through the production of many apparent, *unitary* beings.

I keep emphasizing Parmenides' phrase "apparent beings" because the outline or boundary of each individual entity is only *apparently* real. In truth, every entity in the universe is, just like the Buddhists believe, completely dependent for its existence on every other entity. There is no real separation. When we reach the level of consciousness on which we can perceive with our minds and feel with our hearts the Unity of Being itself, we will know and feel how this is so. The totality of Being is so subtly balanced that every change affects the whole, and therefore every change affects every other thing. And every individual thing in existence is *supported* by the consciousness of other beings that hold it in existence *as* that particular thing.

Now consciousness itself is an expression of the Unity of Being. Being itself is fundamentally pure awareness, pure mind. That vast crystalline, shining sphere is an image of a pure consciousness—consciousness as it is in itself, untarnished with things to be aware of. It is aware precisely of itself, of its own perfect nature. But that very fact—that it is aware of itself—is the principle by which we ourselves create with *our* consciousness the many things we experience in the world. In every moment we create the whole, by envisioning things one at a time.

Now you can understand what I mean when I say that consciousness actually creates reality. I mean just this: that our minds create the outlines, the boundaries, the identities of the things we are aware of. And each time we do this, we are in fact enacting an expression of the one reality, and maintaining in the very production of multitude, the oneness of Being.

The Flower of Life

The highest symbol of the Unity of Being is a perfect, untarnished sphere. Corresponding to this and symbolizing the power of Being to produce a multitude of apparent things, is the figure in Sacred Geometry known throughout the entire universe as the Flower of Life. In *Nothing* I presented the structure of the Flower of Life *(figure 1.2)* in some detail, so here I will merely repeat that it is a figure containing nineteen spheres with equal radii, and that these spheres overlap so that the circumference of one sphere passes through the centers of its neighbors. These spheres are all circumscribed by a single sphere, so the entire structure is derived from the unique sphere itself. All of the figures from sacred geometry: the so-called Platonic solids *(figure 1.3)*, the so-called Kabbalistic Tree of Life, the ratios and proportions of the Fibonacci series and the Golden Mean by which the basic structures of all life and consciousness can be comprehended —all these things can be simply and elegantly derived by geometrical operations performed on the Flower of Life. If you are interested in seeing how this is so I strongly recom-

Figure 1–2. The Flower of Life.

mend that you look them up in *Nothing* and, with a compass
and straight edge, make your own experiments with draw-
ing the figures I describe there.

For our present purposes, we are concerned with one particular figure derived from the Flower of Life (although later
on I will be talking about the Kabbalistic Tree of Life as well),
the figure I mentioned above known as the Merkaba. The
key to the Merkaba figure is the star tetrahedron—two inter-
locking tetrahedrons inscribed within a sphere. A tetrahedron is a four-sided pyramid, and when interlocked and placed
within a sphere with the points of the pyramids touching the

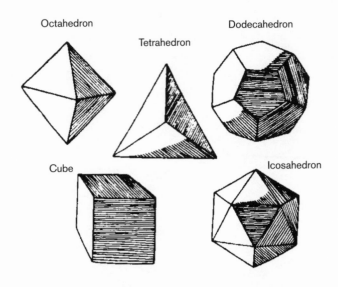

Octahedron

Tetrahedron

Dodecahedron

Cube

Icosahedron

Figure 1–3. The five Platonic solids.

sphere's circumference, you have something that looks like a three-dimensional Star of David. This figure in fact is the very form of the Unity of Being from the point of view of its capacity to create the many apparent entities in the world. When you arrive at Christ Consciousness—the dimensional level on which the Unity of Being can be experienced directly and felt, not only understood, to be the truth—you will be able to see and feel how in fact every individual thing in the universe has its own Merkaba.

Actually, there is a little more to this figure that needs to be described before we can see how and in what way each item has its own Merkaba. Running through the center of the star tetrahedron figure, from the top of the upward pointing pyramid to the bottom of the one that points downward, is a central channel or tube that continuously receives energy —*prana*—from above and below. This constant flow establishes on an energetic level the connection of each thing with the Unity of Being. When we successfully complete the practice, which I described in *Nothing* and repeated again in *Something*, for becoming aware our own Merkaba, we experience two vast fields of force rotating in opposite directions, centered at the base of the spine, extending about fifty-five feet out in physical space away from our bodies. This counter-rotating force field is our Merkaba energy field. Every planet and every galaxy, indeed every distinct object that anyone has ever been aware of, has, when seen with the subtle vision of higher dimensional awareness, a Merkaba energy field that is its connection with the Unity of Being and acts as a conduit to the unlimited energy that belongs to Being itself.

Now since ultimately Being itself is unique, there is really only one Merkaba, only one energy field. So when one becomes aware of one's own Merkaba or of the energy fields surrounding other objects, one is actually at that moment aware of the Unity of Being itself. At that point you can tap into its unlimited power because you no longer experience any difference between yourself and Being. You are not *a* being, you are Being itself. You do not *have* Unity, you *are* unity. For to be and to be one, says Aristotle, are the same.

The Universe as a Hologram

Contemporary physics, though a product of materialistic and exclusively left-brain thinking, often has very interesting insights into certain aspects of reality. If we approach these insights in the right way, they can help us in developing our own more intuitive approach. From time to time I will bring in ideas from science, not because I think that these represent anything like an authoritative picture of reality, but because they can help us in this way. It is also true that their presence in our culture indicates that in some sense concepts from a higher dimensional reality are beginning to penetrate our world.

An area of physics that may help us understand something about the Unity of Being is the science of the hologram.

A hologram is a kind of photographic image that contains much more information than an ordinary photograph: it can represent an object as a solid entity so that as you move around it different sides of it come into view. A moving hologram can be a replica of a living being, or set up a room or scene inside of which it is possible to walk around just as if the place were really there. In principle, a hologram can reproduce the visual qualities of anything whatsoever. How come? Because what we think of as being really "there" in a "real" room or scene is actually the presence of certain configurations of "information" that create the appearances that we experience as that room or scene. Reproduce the information, and you reproduce the appearance. This, incidentally, is how computers are able to create "virtual reality."

The hologram itself doesn't just hold a simple image of the thing it is a picture of the way a photonegative does. Rather, the information is encoded all over the hologram at once. The entire image can be recreated from a tiny portion of it. If you break the hologram in half, you don't lose half the image. It's all still there.

In the 1980s, the brain physiologist Karl Pribram and the physicist David Bohm began to think about the human mind on the one hand and the universe on the other as being like holograms.

Karl Pribram discovered that memory stored as information in the human brain is not held down in specific places but seems to be spread out like the information in a hologram. In certain cases, when a part of the brain is destroyed in an accident or through surgery, other parts of the brain are able to compensate and restore the missing information.

Information is stored "non-locally." *All* the information is stored *all over* the brain. It is as if the information were in some way more real than the physical vehicle that contains it; as if what we really are is not our physical body at all, but the information that describes what our bodies appear to be. And what is true of our physical bodies may be true of the material universe as a whole, for the phenomenon of non-locality in the brain has a corresponding phenomenon in the universe at large, showing a remarkable coincidence between the human organ connected with knowledge and that about which the brain has knowledge: the universe itself.

It turns out in quantum physics, according David Bohm, that the information involved in the interaction between sub-atomic particles—electrons, protons, neutrons, and scores of other particles now known to physicists—is not only contained in the particles themselves, but in some mysterious but precisely calculable way exists at all points in space. In other words, the information of the universe is not "local"—it is not limited to the specific place where things occur. You can get a sense of this if you think about the way the image of an object or a scene is contained by a beam of light. When light strikes a rabbit running across a field, the information that is the image of that rabbit is reflected throughout space so that if you have a lens strong enough and sharp enough, you can focus the image of that rabbit anywhere that the light extends. The human eye might not be able to see the rabbit at all from more than, say, one-hundred feet away. But an eagle would be able to see it from a comparably much greater distance. The only difference is in the properties of the lenses in the eyes of the human and the eagle. The image itself pervades space and only requires the right lens to pick it up. Similarly, surveillance cameras placed in satellites can pick up detailed information about what is going on between humans on Earth hundreds of miles below.

Now astonishingly, what is true of images and light, is actually true of everything that happens in the universe whatsoever: all the information about the universe is in fact simultaneously present everywhere. In a sense, whatever is really happening is happening "non-locally." Simple location is just the way things appear to us because of our limited ability to access information. The whole world is like a hologram: everything that is happening anywhere, in fact is happening everywhere!

Here we are talking about physical phenomena in our three-dimensional universe, at the dimensional level that is accessible to us since the fall of Atlantis. Even on this level, though we experience things as happening in a separated and local manner, we can discover, through scientific analysis, that things are not really separate or local at all. In fact, these physical phenomena are dim reflections of the much greater truth that exists throughout all dimensions of reality—the Unity of Being itself—the fact that we were speaking about a little earlier, that though things appear to be many, in fact there is only a single reality that generates infinitely varied appearances of itself throughout all dimensions everywhere.

Soliton Waves

The entire universe, according to the Melchizedeks, is a vast structure of energies. Ordinary contemporary physics also sees the cosmos as built entirely of energies, albeit interpreted in a materialistic and thoroughly left-brain manner. And psychologists for at least a century have thought of the human psyche as being driven by "psychic energy." But thinking that the world is made entirely of energy may help us break our own materialistic habits, and help us change our view of who and what we are. It may be helpful to think about how even our ordinary material reality can actually by seen as made of nothing but waves of energy.

All the solid things of our world—buildings and mountains and computer chips and human bodies—are actually complex composites of many different kinds of waves.

Remember, each individual thing, to a person living in higher dimensional realities, is unified by its own Merkaba energy field, which is both what gives it its individuality and unites it to all other things. So we might say that anything whatsoever is a complex wave that organizes and harmonizes all the lesser waves that come together in and through it. Such an organizing wave or wave form is called a *soliton wave*. A soliton wave comprises and holds together many subordinate wave forms, and gives the keynote or fundamental character for the system of waves under its sway. Complex entities like human bodies or galaxies or overtones of dimensions are made up of simpler systems of waves. But at whatever level we look, there is really nothing but waves and waves within waves—Merkaba energy fields contained within greater Merkaba energy fields.

For instance, the human body seems to be made of solid and liquid substances—sinew and bone, lymph and blood. But actually each aspect of the body has a characteristic rhythmic pulse. A rhythmic pulse or a recurrent cycle is the same thing as a vibrational frequency. Frequency just means how frequently a pulse or a cycle recurs. The frequency of the rotation of the Earth is one cycle every twenty-four hours. In the body, the most familiar pulses are given by the frequency of the beat of the heart, the rhythm of the breath, and the menstrual cycle. But there is also the rhythm in which the ventricles of the brain emit cerebro-spinal fluid, and there are the various frequencies of brain waves and the many cycles which produce and dissolve the innumerable biochemical substances that constitute our biological existence. And beyond all this, every organ, even every cell, emits tiny electromagnetic fields that pulsate at rates special to their kind and to themselves; and beyond that, each atom is held in electro-magnetic equilibrium between the different vibratory properties of the particles and waves of which it is formed. In short, our bodies are not made of bones and sinews and fluids at all, but of the coordination of these innumerable rhythms and wave forms, all orchestrated into a vast harmony, a symphony of vibrant life. Scientists are beginning to think of our bodies in this way, and the idea that there is a single wave or frequency that organizes all of these wave-forms is beginning to take hold. The biology and medicine of the future will be a science of wave-forms.

What is true of our material nature is true of our spiritual nature, of the multi-dimensional structure of our cosmos, and of the whole of Being itself. Everything is waves and waves within waves, waves crossing waves, waves over-mastering waves. There is a wave form that encompasses each of our lives in time—a single pulse that begins with our birth and fades away with our death—and a larger more extensive wave that encompasses and includes our individual life in a greater life-being, that flows from life to life and travels to and through us from dimensions unknown. It is this greater life that is our individual Merkaba field and of which we need to become aware. These higher dimensional waves do not move in time in the same way that all the biological rhythms do, but encompass our beings in a way that it is impossible to imagine without experiencing them for ourselves. But a door to expanding our consciousness to our higher-dimensional wave-forms is to experience our physical bodies in terms of their pulsations and energies.

The Nature of Polarity

If we were actually able to perceive ourselves and our world entirely in terms of interacting wave forms, we would see that there is no real separation between ourselves and our world, or between ourselves and each other, or between all the different things in the world. Everything flows into and merges with everything else. Boundaries are perceived. Limits appear. But in reality, everything pulsates and radiates beyond its boundary and interacts with the radiant energy emanating from everything else in its neighborhood. Our tendency to divide the world up into solid chunks makes it possible to imagine that we could remake the world according to what we think is good and what is bad, that we could select which chunks we want to have near us and which ones we want to eliminate. But from the perspective of a universe of energies, this doesn't make any sense at all. When we decide that something is bad and that we want to reject it or exclude it, we actually send out a wave of negative energy that mixes in our environment and darkens our own reality. We contract our minds and our bodies in order to emit these dark rays of rejection. Our acts of judging become parts of our world. They do not really succeed in eliminating the things we think are evil. They only increase our own unhappy state.

The attitude of mind that sees the things of the world as divided up into separate entities and then judges these entities as good or bad is called "dualism" or "Polarity Consciousness." When the mind and heart together become aware of the Unity of Being, there is an end to this dualistic vision. What is this vision? What, if anything, is "wrong" with it? Actually there can be nothing really "wrong" with dualism as such, for to think that there is something wrong with it is in itself entirely dualistic!

Dual-ism means "two-ism": seeing the whole of Being as somehow fundamentally *di-vided*. (The word "di-vided" itself means "seeing two." "Di" like "duo" means "two," and "–vided" means "seen." "–vided" is related to "vision.") There are many kinds of dualism, many ways in which the mind has of creating "dichotomies." ("Di-chotomoy" means "cut in two.") It is the most natural thing in the world for the three-dimensional mind to create dichotomies, divisions, dualities. We see things in terms of left and right, up and down, hot and cold, big and small, more and less. There are many powerful philosophical systems that are based on very broad and general dualities. The philosophy of the 17th century French thinker, Rene Descartes, which influenced the development of modern scientific thought, claimed that all of reality can be divided into two absolutely different kinds of "stuff": a kind of stuff called "thinking stuff" that is conscious and intelligent and that is not really located in time and space, has no materiality, and is immortal; and a kind of stuff called "extended stuff," stuff that takes up time and space: matter.

The kind of dualism that I am most concerned with and that quite disappears as soon as one catches a glimpse of the truth of the Unity of Being, is the dualism between good and evil: the view of reality as divided not only or most importantly between different kinds of stuff, but as a great, polarized, cosmic struggle between ultimately opposed forces or tendencies, or between two great beings: God and Satan or Lucifer. This too is a natural tendency of third-dimensional mind: to divide everything we see or know, everything we feel, everything we think, as tending toward the good or tending toward the evil. This kind of "moral dualism" (and indeed all kinds of dualism) is actually a rather direct *consequence* of the tendency to divide, dichotomize, to distinguish. We distinguish that which is good for us as opposed to bad for us, but first of all because we distinguish *us!* We separate *our* kind of being from everything that is not us.

Once we have separated Americans, or Christians, or white people, or black people, or men, or women, or any group whatsoever as being "*our* group" as opposed to all the rest of the human family, we want to support the survival of our group, and we don't care that much about the rest. We divide humanity into "us" and "them," or "me" and "not me." We think that our survival, our prosperity, our success is "good," and anything that opposes it or resists it, is "evil." Notice how dichotomizing—cutting the whole into two parts —happens on many levels. First I divide myself from the rest of humanity. If I expand my view, perhaps I identify myself with my family. Now there is my family versus all the other families. If I expand my view a little further, the "good guys" are the clan or nationality to which my family belongs or the corporation for which I work or the religion that I was brought up in. Now I am in competition with other clans or companies, or potentially at war with other nations. And as for religion, certainly my religion must be uniquely in possession of the true and the good, and the other religions must be false and evil.

If I am truly sophisticated, I might identify myself not with this or that group but with the entire human race. But that doesn't end dualism at all, because now I have divided the humans from every other kind of being: animals, spirits, extraterrestrial or other-dimensional entities, plants, minerals, the Earth or the galaxy, or, finally Being as a whole. At any level whatsoever, if one stops and says "I am a Christian, I am a human, I am an Earthling, I am a living being ... " just where one stops, short of the whole of Being itself, has created a division, a dichotomy, and one is naturally going to think of one's own side of the dichotomy as "good" and the other as, if not absolutely "evil," at least not as good, not as important, not as worthy of survival, prosperity, or salvation.

So the entire business of good and evil, together with the anxiety for the survival of oneself, or one's own group or category or clan, is the result of the way things appear to us on the third-dimensional level, i.e., as made of separate, individual things and assemblages of things. We do not see the whole, or if we catch a glimpse of it, it seems to be a whole made up of many individual, separated parts. Division, and consequently duality, runs through our entire way of seeing Being. When we pass beyond the third dimension, this tendency toward division, toward seeing things as separate entities, dissolves. We not only see Being as a whole, we feel ourselves to *be* that whole! It is not even that we see ourselves as *part* of the whole—that is still to think dualistically, since the relationship "part/whole" is just another division, another dualism. If we ourselves, each and every one of us, is, in our very Being, the whole of Being, there is no longer any reason whatsoever to divide things into good and evil. Either everything is unimaginably and powerfully positive and good, or the whole question just disappears because it is no longer very interesting to be thinking in terms of good and bad at all. Even the distinction between dualism and the Unity of Being no longer holds, for one sees the possibility of third dimensional existence itself as completely woven into the fabric of Being, and no longer the way it seems to itself, as separated out as a distinct level. It no longer makes any sense at all to think of anything as wrong and therefore to be condemned, cut off, or avoided.

Part II

Burning
with the Fire
of Purpose

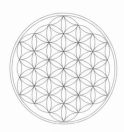

The Shift in Identity

If it is true that we create reality unerringly, how we identify ourselves—what we think we really are—is fundamental to the whole process. If we identify ourselves as powerless and ultimately separated from the rest of Being, then the universe is always going to give back a reflection that's consistent with what we're putting out. The universe is a "universal affirmer": for better or worse it always says "yes" to our thoughts.

If you identify yourself as a powerless victim, it is as if you were giving a command to the universe to behave just as if this were so. The result: the entire universe conforms to that command and says yes to it, and you receive confirmation from it that you have no power. You get what you put out. That's always true. That's how we create reality.

We tend to miss the cause and effect relationship between our thoughts and our world. Very simply, we only see what we expect to see because we are unwittingly, unknowingly, at the effect of our own dysfunctional, unconscious patterns. These patterns are sustained by energy from the past that is stuck in the body and remains there symptomatic of what in Rebirthing are called "incompletions": incomplete emotions, actions, and intentions from past lives, from the trauma of birth, and from childhood.

What is clear is that we need to shift the command we are giving to reality by shifting our identity, our inner image of who we are, from being a victim to being a master, from being an isolated individual being to taking responsibility for Being as a whole.

The purpose of this part of this book is to show you how to shift that command, to begin to identify yourself in a way that gives you access to your full power, your true nature.

Intuition

We are spiritual beings—spiritual masters—from the very beginning. We do not have to change anything in our basic makeup in order to become a master or achieve Enlightenment. We have only to uncover what we actually are and shift our sense of our own identity. Our spiritual being is not anything external. It is not like our DNA or our physical appearance or our personality with its history, its quirks, and its particular makeup. It is entirely an internal matter. This means that there is no way that we can *observe* the fact that we are spiritual masters. There is no "evidence" on the basis of which we can convince ourselves that we are not lowly humans but spiritual beings. The shift in identity must be accomplished, therefore, without our seeking evidence for the fact that it is possible.

This is both the most difficult and most essential point. Shifting our sense of identity is something you simply must *declare.* You are a spiritual being: this is a possibility that you must seize and accept as true, not because you have direct evidence that it is true, and not because you accept it on my authority or because anyone else says so. You must accept it because you have an *intuition*—a hunch, a feeling—that it is true. And you must act from that intuition. Now just what is intuition?

Perhaps you are aware that contemporary brain-biologists know that the brain is divided into two "hemispheres" that perform contrasting functions. The left hemisphere is rational, logical. It wants to know the facts and it makes up its mind on the basis of them and on the basis of logical thinking about them. The right hemisphere is intuitive: it has feelings about things, it grasps situations and realities as a whole. It doesn't search for facts and evidence and it doesn't draw conclusions based on reasoning. It *feels* and it *knows*.

Intuition works in us all to one degree or another. Have you ever walked into a crowded room or a certain neighborhood and suddenly had an apprehensive feeling—a sense that something is amiss? This feeling doesn't arise from your assessing particular facts. It is an impression that comes all at once and as a whole. Such a feeling is an intuition. Now intuitions do not only come in this negative form. Here is a more positive example. You are driving in the country and as the highway turns around a bend, suddenly an incredibly beautiful open view of fields and mountains and sky appears. You are awestruck by its grandeur. This is also an intuition. It doesn't happen because you assess the details of the landscape and judge the colors of the trees, the shapes of the mountains, the expanse of the sky. It happens all at once, and without logical thinking.

In regard to the question of our inner identity, the left and right hemispheres work in contrasting ways. Your left hemisphere is always on the lookout for *evidence* of your personal character. It wants feedback from your teachers or your employers, your friends, your family to assure it that it is superior or at least "okay." It believes in objective tests— IQ tests, standardized aptitude or achievement tests—it measures itself by material success in the form of a high pay check, social status, and so forth. It looks to your accomplishments or your status for facts to determine your identity. It wants the evidence, and it makes a judgment on this basis as to what and who your are.

In contrast, the right hemisphere doesn't require evidence.

It works from an inner feeling, an intuition. It gives you an immediate, *felt sense* of who you are. With it you have immediate knowledge of your inner state, and from it you form a self-image that isn't based on performance or on external traits that can be verified or denied.

People tend to be dominated by one or the other of the two hemispheres and so are more or less prone to judging reality by facts and logic or grasping it as a whole by image and intuition. All human beings have both sides, and both are necessary for life on this planet and in the third dimension, but modern society is very much dominated by left-brain, logical thinking. Our society emphasizes the logical, left-brain functions in its educational institutions. You go to school to learn to read and write, to learn arithmetic, to study the facts of history. Intuition-developing activities like music and art are forever in danger of losing their funding, and meditation or prayer are ruled out altogether. It is as if society can't figure out what to do with intuition. It doesn't know how to value it. The result: we live in a largely fragmented, technocratic world without vision or wholeness. And we tend to be less developed intuitively than logically. We need a good dose of intuition wherever we can find it to set the balance right, because without intuitive thinking we cannot shift our identity from victim to spiritual master.

Of course, not every intuition is a positive one. You can have a positive or a negative self-image, and form positive or negative beliefs about yourself and about reality accordingly. If you believe you are condemned to being a victim and at the effect of circumstance or karma or fate, this belief may be rooted in a negative intuition—an image of the self or the world, or an inner feeling about yourself or the world. So it is not that intuitive, right-braining thinking is good and logical left-brain thinking is bad. But the possibility that you are a spiritual master, a spiritual being having a human experience, is something that you can only grasp intuitively. It comes as an inner response, a sense of personal confirmation. When you read my words, for instance, something inside you may say, "Yes, that's the way it is. I've always known that." This inner confirmation comes from your intuition. It is actually a moment of awakening to your Higher Self. Your Higher Self recognizes the truth when it hears it and steps forth through this intuitive feeling. This is not at all the same as accepting the words of an authority just because the authority asserts it. The latter comes with a feeling of fear, not hope or recognition.

Your Higher Self is not something about which you can gather evidence as to whether or not it exists. It is a *possibility,* something that you grasp with your aspiration and your intention. If you try to find a basis for it as a fact, you will not find it at all. It is not the fact-seeking mind that can ever hope to find it. But when hoping that it exists becomes *intuiting, intending* and finally *declaring* that it exists, you find that its very being lies in that *intuiting,* that *intending* and that *declaring.*

Because the certainty that you are a spiritual being is an intuition, you can't wait for the evidence to start showing up. If you don't believe it intuitively, there is nothing that can ever happen that will prove it to you.

Possibility

We ordinarily think of the world as made up of facts. A fact is something that has already happened, or something that is certain to happen. This morning when I woke up the sun was shining. That's a fact. World War II ended in 1945. An historical fact. The Earth goes around the sun in a little more than three-hundred and sixty-five days. A general fact. Facts are definite, fixed, finished. They are what they are and that's the end of it. Facts give rise to other facts. In a world of facts, nothing really changes. The facts of tomorrow are the result of the facts of today.

Ordinarily we recognize that the world contains a lot more than facts. It contains *possibilities*. Tomorrow it *might* rain, or it might *not* rain. Next year you might win the lottery. It's possible. A possibility is *like* a fact: it too is something quite definite, just like a fact is. But as a matter of fact—it hasn't happened yet. A possibility is something that might come true, but then again it might not. In any case it is not *yet* true. It has to do with the future—with something open—something *not yet* fixed and finished. In a sense, a fact is always in the past. It's over and done with. A possibility is never in the past. It has to do with that towards which we are striving. It relates to our wishes, our hopes, our fears.

The world is made of facts and possibilities, in this ordinary sense. A possibility is a possibility for—a fact: a specific thing or event or occurrence. It is quite definite, quite distinct; it just happens not to have happened yet. Yet the fact that reality consists of possibilities and not only facts points the way to a non-ordinary way of seeing reality—reality from the perspective or point of view of *Possibility itself:* the world not *as* a fixed and finished collection of facts, just waiting to become some other fixed and finished facts, but as open in its very Being toward becoming something *more*.

Shifting our identity from being a victim, always at the effect of circumstances, to that of being a master who sees everything as being at his or her command, has a lot do with shifting our basic view of things from Factuality to Possibility. A person living with victim consciousness sees the world as completely made up of facts and only facts. Even the future seems to be nothing but facts that just happen not to have happened yet. Things are as they are and there's nothing much to be done about it. There is no sense of openness, no sense that things might turn out differently than expected. No sense of—Possibility. But for a master even facts themselves are possibilities. Each new circumstance, each new situation, each new configuration of the facts that make up the world, is a new set of possibilities, new opportunities. To become a master is simply to switch one's view from looking at the world as Factuality to the world as Possibility. For a victim, even possibilities are just mere facts. For a Master, even facts are living possibilities.

To shift one's vision from the vision of facts to the vision of Possibility is to live in a world in which whatever one thinks of is instantaneously real, because one's whole mode of understanding what is real has shifted from Factuality to Possibility. It's not that there are no facts, that nothing really occurs or that nothing is solid. It's that whatever occurs, whatever appears as being real and present, is instantly felt as being full of potentiality: you don't only see what it *is*—you see what it might lead to, what you might make of it, how you might take the opportunities that it offers to bring about a greater good for oneself and for all beings everywhere. In the light of Possibility, every fact becomes like a magic jewel: touch it and it yields a whole new world of things that yet might be.

When I speak of Possibility, I am speaking of a way of looking at reality—or more than that—a way of Being. Possibility is itself a way of taking a stand on Being. I could say, in shifting my identity to being a master, I take a stand in and for Possibility, for Being as Possibility. I no longer see the world as made up of facts and mere possibilities for more facts. I see reality itself as Possibility itself. Since possibilities are not facts, or are not yet facts, there is no *evidence* that could support this new stance. Evidence is made up entirely of facts and reasoning about facts or from facts. But

Possibility is itself outside of the world of facts. So when I shift my identity to being a master, this shift is not based on any kind of factual evidence. I don't look at my life and try to find examples of my behavior or of my experience that would show that I am really a master rather than an ordinary human victim. If I did that, I would be right back in the world of facts and evidence. Instead I step right out of that world into the world of Possibility. The world of Possibility is something that I become aware of by using my right brain —my capacity for intuition and feeling. To grasp a possibility, I must have an intuition—a feeling, a sense of it. To make the shift to being a master, all I really need is an intuition, a sense, a feeling, that that is true. To shift from a world of Factuality to a world of Possibility I don't have to have *evidence*. I have to have an intuition. An intuition of what? That Possibility is possible! That Possibility really is another way of taking reality! That a master is someone who dwells in Possibility, for whom every new fact, every new actual event or occurrence, is just the opening of further possibility, and that such a view of reality is open to *me*.

Werner Erhard says somewhere that reality is like a railroad train rushing down the track. If you want to change reality, it isn't enough to be on the train, or even to be an engineer. The track itself runs straight ahead and there isn't any way you can swerve off the track to change what is going to happen. In order to change reality you have to get out in front of the train and lay down a new set of tracks altogether. A new set of tracks is a new world of Possibility: a new *context* for experiencing the world. But actually I would go a bit further and say yes, the world of facts is like a railroad train going down its track. Even if you build new tracks, however, you're *still* in the world of facts—just changing them around a bit. But the world of Possibility is like an airplane flying in free space. There is no track at all. At every moment you are free to continue your course or change your course. You can fly off at a moment's notice in any direction you can imagine. If you have a feeling you want to zoom higher into the wild blue yonder, your wish is your command! All you have to do is think it, and it is so. This is Possibility—the world of Possibility—the world *as* Possibility—the master's world of higher-dimensional reality, where there is no gap between thought and manifestation.

Prophecy and Possibility

Prophecies are vividly grasped possibilities. Certain specially gifted people—people who can see with higher-dimensional consciousness—can see the possibilities inherent in present facts and declare them as what is going to happen. We tend to think of prophets as people who can see the future—their prophecies tell of facts to come. But in a certain sense this misses the most important thing about prophecies, which is not so much that the prophet sees future facts, but that he sees *with the eye of Possibility:* he sees possibilities inherent in the present; he sees a path—but not only a path of facts: he sees an open space and declares it.

The real function of a prophet is to give a wake-up call. It is like the Chinese proverb: If we don't change direction, we are likely to end up where we are headed! As I said in *Something,* the purpose of the prophet is to be proved wrong!

Context and Content

When we truly awaken to Possibility and to our own possibilities, we discover ourselves to be *at the very source of life.* When we are at the very source of life, we can create a new context for our life, for the life of the planet, and indeed, for all life everywhere. Nothing is true but if you think it. And what you think, if you think it with your whole being, becomes true for the whole of Being. That means that you are a co-creator of reality itself. And what we think together, individually and collectively, is the context for everything that can happen.

So our primary business is to create a new context for existence itself, and first of all for our own existence. But our own existence is just that point where the whole of Being concentrates its forces. We are the way that reality assembles itself into a world. When we create a new context for our life and for life in general, the *content* of that context—the facts of existence—show forth new possibilities, and they themselves become radically realigned. Life's contents re-arranges itself spontaneously as happening now in the context we have created. The circumstances that up to this time have been running our lives and from which we thought our experience of life was derived, now begin to reflect and to be colored by our creative declaration of our new context.

You change the context of your life in a timeless moment, in one over-arching intuition. You grasp reality as a whole and in a new way. Perhaps nothing materially has changed at all, but everything has changed. Everything—good and bad, pleasant and unpleasant, hopeful and ominous—it all becomes part of your path. Nothing *has* to be changed; but everything *is* changed, because *you* have changed. Everything is an opportunity now, an occasion for further awakening.

The timeless moment of awakening need not come as a particularly earth-shattering experience. But it is a moment when you realize that you have an awesome responsibility, since you see that you yourself are creating the entire of reality. This responsibility is not a matter of assuming a moral duty, but of literally seizing responsibility as an act of joy. Joyously seizing responsibility for context realigns content.

The context is nothing but a thought, an intention. But when you think that thought; when you hold it in your intention with all of your being, without consideration or hesitation, everything changes. And not for you alone, but for all of life everywhere.

Now the content of your life is no longer running your life. The tail is no longer wagging the dog.

Wake up, take a stand, take responsibility for who you are and why you are here, and the entire universe will re-arrange itself to accommodate your picture of reality. Now you are no longer a helpless victim in life, you are a force of creation. And you are in alignment with the creative process of the universe.

Clearing the Slate

Shifting your identity from victim to master; joyously seizing responsibility; changing the context of existence itself; changing the context of the content of your life: how can all this be done? First, by recognizing that at the bottom of your being both you yourself and the universe itself are a vast *blank slate,* an empty page, a magic writing pad, on which anything can be written. Second, by cleaning your slate of all dysfunctional patterns and incompletions; and third, by declaring your intention to shift your identity from being a powerless victim to being a spiritual master.

So first of all, you need to understand that you are not the *content* of your life: you are a blank slate, a magic writing pad. Your Higher Self is pure Possibility, and as such a conscious context-creator. Your true nature is the immense potentiality of what can be written on the magic writing pad of what you are. And the content of what gets written on your magic writing pad is your thoughts and feelings and actions. The universe itself is a universal affirmer, a universal responder that always says yes to your thoughts. It allows you to write what you will on the blank slate of your nature. And it responds to what you write.

If your thoughts and feelings and actions arise uncon-sciously, you are going to create a reality that's a mirror image of your incompletions—the half-realized intentions, unfin-ished relationships, blocked desires, and unexpressed re-sponses that are left as half-articulate scribblings on your magic writing pad. If they just sit there, unlooked at and unread, they still will shape and condition your world.

Waking up—becoming more conscious—means becom-ing aware of these chaotic inscriptions, these incompleted patterns; but much more importantly, it means seeing that you have the capacity to "clean the slate" and return to an empty, blank state of pure potentiality, pure Possibility. This capacity is actually there at every moment, so you never have to be at these patterns' mercy. You can create your world however you want it right now, by instantaneously wiping the slate clean. You can inscribe whatever you want on the blank slate of your being.

(Practically speaking, for most of us, there is a good bit of work we have to do to get rid of our old patterns. Though the empty slate is always there, finding it beneath all the "stuff" that we have written on it may take some doing. This is what Rebirthing is all about. But in principle, you don't have to wait for anything, to discover the empty state at the center of your being.)

Since our higher nature is our pure potentiality, waking up to our higher nature is not about becoming aware of some kind of ready-made super-person with fantastic characteris-tics and mystical powers. The mystical powers are there—if you declare them. The fantastic personal characteristics will manifest—if you create them, if you inscribe them on the blank slate of your being. Spiritual awakening, enlightenment, rising to a higher dimensional level, discovering Unity Consciousness or Christ Consciousness—all these are about discovering that you have the power to create your own personality and your own life circumstances because you are at bottom an empty state of pure potentiality. If you expect to find something inside yourself that already has a perfectly developed *content,* you are going to be disappointed. It is not the content that always already exists in a perfect state. It is the capacity to create the context. That capacity is what you truly are. And you are always that. And you are already that. Timelessly. At every moment.

The Miracle of Unknowing

Knowledge that you are a blank slate is the highest knowledge. We are conscious context-creators. That is the potentiality of our inner nature. But to realize that potentiality you have to clean the slate: you have to bring your sense of who you are to ground zero—to the empty place where it seems that you are nothing at all. No particular characteristics define you. You are just there, pure being, pure, immediate, present existence.

No matter what the content of your life, no matter how successful or fortunate you think you are, until you know that apart from your power to create your own context, your being is quite empty and meaningless, you don't really know the secret even of your own happiness! Sometimes success and good fortune actually stand in the way of our seeing what we truly are. While we are happy, we don't want to look inside. Not that there is anything wrong with success and good fortune—far from it. It is just that if we are not aware that our present good fortune is the unerring result of our thoughts and attitudes, we will not know how to insure that our happiness continues. For the content of our reality is always unerringly the result of what we have written and what we are writing on our inner writing pad, and if we do not know that, you can be sure that eventually unconscious patterns that already exist will manifest or patterns that we are right now forming will take effect and spoil the party! The only way to insure that the positive contents of your life will remain positive is by taking responsibility for the context in which they are formed, and that involves seeing that at bottom your very being is a blank slate, an empty potentiality.

For the most part we remain ignorant of our true nature because we are unwittingly at the effect of our unconscious, incomplete patterns. Your incompletions cover your inner writing pad, so that it seems you are something quite definite, with fixed personal qualities, thought patterns, and attitudes. It is only by wiping that inner writing pad clean that you can see that you are free to create reality as you will.

In Rebirthing, the point of becoming aware of incompletions and old patterns and allowing stuck energy to surface is not so much to become familiar with the content of the past, as it is to allow the old contents finally to be washed away. That is why we say in Rebirthing that "re-creation is disappearance." We consciously re-create the content of the past by becoming conscious of it and allowing it to integrate, i.e., we allow it to disappear, to dissolve, so that we can re-claim our inner space—the inner blank slate—of our true being. We actually pass from a state of *knowing too much*— of being at the effect of the way we "knew" reality to be— to being in a state of openness and *unknowing*—a state of pure readiness that does not prejudge the oncoming rush of new events by imposing upon them old patterns of thought and feeling, but is ready to enter into new circumstances with a fresh perspective, with the only knowledge that really matters—that whatever happens, we are the creators of the context it happens in.

There is a Korean Zen master named Seung Sahn (Korean Zen is called Chogye) whose whole teaching comes down what he calls "Don't Know Mind." He tries to create situations for the student so that the student has to confront the experience of being *utterly at a loss*—to experience in his very bones the reality that he *doesn't know*—and right in that experience of *not knowing* there is a profound experience of waking up! We wake up right inside of our experience of not knowing by not grasping, not letting our mental patterns take hold of the mind. *This* is the experience of enlightenment— which is really the experience of the Higher Self. It happens completely spontaneously. And why shouldn't it? Since there is really nothing at all in the way of the higher aspects of our nature except our habitual patterns of thought and the stuck energy that resides behind them.

Intention

Once your slate is clean, or even once you have a glimpse of what a clean slate is really like; i.e., once you recognize that you yourself *are* a clean slate, the possibility of creating your own reality will become very clear to you. Now the question is, how can you in practice change your context and shift your identity. The key is intention, 100% intention: the unconditional resolve to make the desired change, to put all your power behind your intention, to declare what it is you intend, and to back your declaration 100%.

Putting your power behind your declaration establishes your intention. Intention in this sense is not ordinary intention. Ordinarily we do things intentionally in a semi-conscious, even half-hearted way. It's Saturday morning and I have planned to go the supermarket to buy food for dinner, but then a friend calls up and suggests that we go bowling. My intention changes. The intention I am speaking of is not like that. It is 100% intention, an all or nothing affair. Either you are a spiritual master or you are powerless victim. There's no half-way position, no "perhaps later when I feel like it I'll think of myself as a spiritual master."

Anything less than 100% intention is the equivalent of zero. This actually has implications not only for the one's evolution as a spiritual being, but for practical, ordinary intention as well. A person with 99% intention is eventually not going to do what they proclaim they are going to do. For instance, say you have decided to lose weight. You think you really want to take off thirty pounds. You decide that you are going to stop eating candy bars and greasy food and that you are going to start a regimen of exercise. But in the back of your mind you are quite attached to candy bars, and you really want to spend your evenings *watching* basketball games rather than shooting hoops at the gym. You want to lose weight but your intention is not 100%. All kinds of considerations and contrary desires are still active in you, so as soon as an opportunity to go off your diet or skip an evening of exercise arises, your intention falters. Soon you have forgotten your intention pretty much, and you experience yourself as a failure—you have failed in your intent. Now you start looking for all the reasons why either it is okay that you failed, or that you were helpless victim and couldn't "help yourself." But the real reason was simply that your intention was divided to begin with. When you declare your intention, even for something practical like losing weight, and you do it 100%, you can see in advance the candy bars and basketball games that you will have to forego in order to fulfill it. You see it and agree to it. Now when "temptations" arise they are not a threat. You remain in contact with your intention and you succeed quite naturally.

It is natural that, whenever you form a firm intention to do something—even when that intention is 100%—that all of your alternative desires will rise up and appear before you. This is true most surely when your intention is a spiritual ideal. Anything within you that is less pure than that intention can and will arise, and when it does it will serve as *evidence* for you to give your intention up. Any time you take a stand, any time you make a declaration that's based on pure and powerful ideals, you can count on the fact that anything less pure that you are still holding onto—your doubts and considerations—are still going to come to your attention. Now if your ideal itself is based on *evidence*, if it is based on left-brain thinking, then all these doubts will present counter-evidence and force you to waver in your ideal. This is why your declaration that you are spiritual master must come from a place that is beyond evidence: it is so because you say so, because you have an intuition that comes from the very core of your nature that it is true. It is not based on arguments or facts. So when arguments or facts that seem to prove that you are a powerless victim and not a spiritual master arise, they will have no force.

Attitude

The way that intention translates into action is through *attitude*. In aeronautics, the *attitude* of an airplane's wing is the tilt or angle which makes the plane fly upward or downward. With a sharply angled upward *attitude*, the plane soars towards the heavens. With a sharply angled downward *attitude*, the plane heads down to the ground. The *attitude* of the wing is the way the pilot controls the plane: it translates his *intention* into *action*.

Similarly our own inner attitude turns our inner intention into action in our lives and in our world. If we have the attitude of a victim, it is as if we were assuming the bodily and mental posture that naturally tends towards being at the

effect of circumstances. We are shallow breathers, we hunch
our shoulders, we develop a slouching posture, as if we were
already half-way to the grave. If we have the attitude of a
spiritual master, our posture will be straight and balanced.
Like an ascending airplane, our lives will naturally tend toward
higher-dimensional reality, and we will experience our ability to determine our own reality consciously according to our
own desires. In both cases, attitude follows intention, and
therefore the reality that we experience—the result of our
attitude—is the result of our thoughts and feelings. For our
attitude is nothing but the expression of our habitual thoughts
and feelings.

Attitude expresses intention. If our intention is at the
effect of our incompleted thoughts and emotions from the
past, we will be at the effect of those incompletions. Why are
they incompletions? What is incomplete about them? When
we are impacted by something powerful in our lives, it is as
though we are receiving a blast of energy from the environment. Often this happens in such a way that all we can do is
try to guard ourselves against the incoming force by con-
tracting our muscles and setting up a defensive posture in
our minds. We form an attitude that is intended to ward off
the blow. The consequence is that the incoming energy strikes
against the tough resistant surface we have created in our
bodies and in our minds.

Now energy always has the form of a wave. It is a continuous movement with its own intensity and measure. Energy
cannot be destroyed. It cannot be stopped. If you put up a
powerful barrier to block an incoming force, that force has
to go somewhere. If the barrier is our contracted muscles, the
energy passes into the muscles and gets stuck there. At the
same time the thoughts and emotions that we were experiencing while we were bracing against the incoming blow also
gets stuck. We have an incomplete intention—an attitude—

that remains associated with the energy stuck in our body where we braced.

An intention is incomplete when it doesn't have a chance to express itself fully at the moment when it was formed. It remains as a general form of rage or frustration, for instance —as an inarticulate cry against the outrage that is being committed against us. So what gets stuck in our body is an incomplete gesture, an unfinished action, connected with an unexpressed thought of outrage. And all this remains within our bodies and forms an unconscious and *suppressed* part of our inner world. At the same time, the energy, the thoughts, and the emotions we were resisting get *preserved* by the very contraction with which we resisted them. *Resistance equals persistence.* We cause the persistence of that which we resist.

The source of suppression and resistance is actually Polarity Consciousness, but Polarity Consciousness is something entirely inside us. We ourselves produce it as the lens or filter through which we perceive the outer world and which separates us from it. What in us is making us apply the "polarity filter" rather than declaring Unity Consciousness? It is the incompletions from the past that we sustain living inside us in the form of stuck energy. So let us look a little more closely at what these incompletions are.

The Incompletion of Birth Trauma

When we are born into the third-dimensional world, we are physically helpless beings. We have almost no control over our physical movements. While we were in the womb, our breath came to us from our mother's body, and now we must learn to breathe on our own. We are thrown into a place that is controlled by adult human beings with a language and all kinds of ways of doing things about which we know nothing. We have no way of feeding ourselves, protecting ourselves from the dangers of the physical world, or keeping ourselves warm, without the help of these other human beings. We are profoundly *incomplete*. We lack what we need for our own survival. Everything in us is geared to merely staying alive.

The first confusion we experience as we emerge into the third-dimensional world is that even though we are multidimensional, *spiritual* beings, we find ourselves at the effect of the trauma and shock of being thrown into a third-dimensional, *human* world. And we *identify* with the condition under which we find ourselves. Because that condition is *as* an incomplete, dependent being, we begin to feel that *we* are incomplete. Because that condition demands a total focus on mere survival, our mind begins believe that its only function is to assist in that survival. Survival is all. The mind thinks that its only concern is survival, and not only that, the mind becomes concerned with its *own* survival. As it develops it develops an ego. It comes to identify with its own limited ideas and eventually learns to defend itself by resisting ideas and opinions other than its own. At birth, the mind is a multisensory record of all that is happening to us. It retains the traces of the pain of coming into the world and the frustration of all that happened to it while it was dependent for survival. We come to identify and remain identified with those traces of trauma in our mind.

The conditions of our birth are made much worse by the actual practices that in our society usher us into the world. The concern of the adults ought to be to show the newborn infant that the outside world is a safe and exciting place, and that it has all it needs to live harmoniously within it. But what do they do? At the very first moment of life they show turmoil and tension. Instead of allowing the infant to make the transition from prenatal breathing to direct breathing through the lungs, they violently force it to begin breathing all at once by severing its umbilical cord and whacking it on the behind, so that its first breath is a howl of terror and dismay. Instead of welcoming it with loving care and allowing it to come into the world in its own good time, they surround it with impatient medical professionals, tug it out of the womb with unfeeling forceps, and if it won't come out speedily enough to suit their convenience, they perform a Cesarean section and basically rip it out of its mother's belly. These initial experiences scar us all. The intensity and details of the experience differ from person to person, but we all carry the energetic trace of the terror and violence with which we came into the world. This lies at the very basis of our minds, and, since we create our world unerringly out of the contents of our mind, it's no wonder that our world is full of ignorance, terror, and violence.

The energy of the traumatic experience of birth is not something that we can assimilate and integrate at the time that we are born. To do that would require an understanding and intelligence that, under third-dimensional conditions, we do not have until we are mature human beings. The consequence is that the energy gets stuck in our bodily tissues, and the incomplete thoughts that accompany them remain inside us and echo again and again in our later lives.

These echoes recur in our being when circumstances arise that in any way remind us of the circumstances where they were formed. The voice of the obstetrician, the odors of the hospital, the feeling of being handled by cold, unfeeling, anxious, medical hands—even things said by medical practitioners or others at the scene of our birth—remain locked inside us. And when smells or voices or words occur in later life that are like them, the traumatic energies of our birth are reawakened and play havoc with our emotional lives. As long as we unconsciously identify with these suppressed emotions and as long as the stuck energy of birth trauma remains locked in our bodies, we will experience the evidence of the fact that we are completely at the effect of our unconscious minds.

To recover our Higher Self and liberate our mind from its identification with the limiting conditions of its birth into the third dimension, the energy that was awakened during these traumatic events must be released. The breathing technique of Rebirthing is designed to release that energy and therefore liberate the mind from the forms of thought that came into place in the ignorance of our violent beginnings.

Incompletions from Past Lives

As spiritual beings we did not just come into existence with our birth. We have lived many lives before this one under not very different third-dimensional conditions. We have lived many times before, and we have died many times before. And very often the conditions under which we passed from our previous lives involved other kinds of incompletion: incomplete emotional reactions, incomplete relationships, and unfulfilled intentions. If we died under violent circumstances, the terror and rage connected with our death would have had no chance of completing itself. Emotion is a wave of energy, and if our life is cut off while we are in a state of emotional excitation, the intensity of that wave remains lodged in our being. If we died in a rage, that rage will continue in our future existence. Again, if we died during an unresolved quarrel, we would carry a sense of the incomplete relationship with us. Just as the energy from birth trauma lodges in our tissues and remains suppressed until released, so do these incompletions from past lives live on in us.

Finally, if we formed a strong intention to achieve some action and died without completing it, the energy of that intention will continue to affect us until the intention is carried out.

Incompletions from Childhood

Since as human beings living in the third dimension we take many years to mature, the early years of our life are very powerful in forming attitudes, thoughts, and patterns that continue to affect us in later life. In the same way that birth trauma freezes energy in our tissue and incomplete emotions, relationships, and intentions continue to exert pressure on our present life, so do incomplete emotions and intentions from childhood continue to exist as stuck energy within us.

The mechanism by which energy gets stuck in our tissue is through the control of our breathing. It works like this. When we feel a strong emotion, a bodily command is issued for the expenditure of energy. Say you are walking on the street about to open the door to your apartment. You are tapped on the shoulder by a mugger with a knife who demands your purse or your wallet. Your heart starts beating a mile a minute: your instinct is to fight or to run. Your adrenal glands pump hormones into your blood to mobilize energy. Once energy is aroused you have to have oxygen to burn it. You have to breathe. But say in this case you don't run. You see the mugger's open knife, you sense his violent rage. You are terrified, frozen. You feel your chest tighten. You contract your muscles to suppress the impulse to fight or flee, and you hold your breath to assist in this process of suppression.

What happens in the case of extreme threat occurs at a less intense level every time you experience an emotion of any kind and do not immediately express it. Your muscles contract to block the impulse to act; you subtly hold your breath in order to block the expenditure of energy. You body and your psyche retain the energy traces of these events of blocking, contraction, and suppression.When circumstances similar to the ones that wakened the energy arise, the stuck energy has a chance to come out. So you have to hold your breath and contract your muscles again. Over time, these efforts to control your breath become habitual. You become shallow in your breathing, ineffective and hesitant in your actions.

Resistance = Persistence

Suppression doesn't work in the long run. It is a form of resistance, and resistance always fosters the persistence of what we resist. Often we literally become that which we are trying to push away. For instance. Many young people decide that they never want to become like their parents. But it is natural to absorb some of the characteristics of the people we live with, so the resolve not to become like our parents requires resistance. Resistance takes energy. To resist becoming like our mother or our father creates a counter-force molded to the fit of the characteristics we are trying to hold at bay. Those characteristics become a part of us by the very fact that we have to exert all this precisely focused energy in order to avoid them. So in this sense, we have caused the persistence of our parent's personality by resisting it.

Usually we form these strong, resistant resolves while we are young, and then more or less forget about them. They remain, nevertheless, as unconscious fixtures in our minds. As we grow up and make friends and alliances with other people, those unconscious fixtures go to work. Even though they represent traits that we don't like, they are nonetheless very familiar to us and have become parts of ourselves; and we are naturally drawn to people who have them. Now suddenly we find we have friends or associates or even husbands and wives who exhibit precisely those personality traits that we had sworn so adamantly that we didn't want any part of! So in this second way, our resistance has become the persistence in our lives of just what we were trying to avoid.

If we didn't resist those traits to begin with, we would naturally absorb some of them in a form that is modified by our own personality. If they did recur, they'd no longer be our parents' traits but our own. But more often than not they'd change and become something else, simply dissolving into our own history. Again, resistance creates persistence.

In general, avoiding and denying, i.e. suppressing the incompletions of our past are forms of resistance. Once resisted they live on in the body as stuck energy and have the potential to create emotional disturbance. Perhaps during times when life is going along at a regular pace it is possible to keep the incompletions of the past suppressed without causing any undue stress or psychological difficulty. But that is not true today. We live in accelerated times. One of the consequences of the Sirians' having decided to speed up the evolution of the planet [see Part III] in order to get us through the difficulty of the solar eruption of 1972, is that we are all evolving at an incredible rate. This means that a tremendous amount of creative energy is available to us and is flowing through our system, stirring up any energy blocked within our bodies. It is simply not possible to hold that energy down. Whatever is in us is bound to come out, and if we continue to resist it, we do so at our peril.

A Setting of Safety and Trust

When we shift our identity and declare that we are spiritual beings and abandon thinking in terms of good and evil, right and wrong, our inner space expands to include that which previously we have been excluding by suppression. It is just such dualistic thinking that makes the exclusion, suppression, and ignorance of our true nature possible. Safety and trust can only come from a declaration that you are a spiritual being, i.e., by changing your context and intuitively shifting your identity. When you perform this shift suppression is no longer necessary. There is plenty of room to handle whatever comes your way, internally or externally, because you are no longer stuck in an attitude of judging things good and bad.

Polarity Consciousness both derives from and fosters a context of suppression, resistance and ignorance. In such a context we are always in a state of fear, for of course we are apprehensive that whatever might happen internally or externally might be harmful, wrong, or evil. Whenever fear takes over you go into a contracted state, and that leads to more resistance, and you just go round and round in a vicious circle. Nothing can break that circle but your decision—your 100% intention—simply to step out of it: to declare that you are already a spiritual being whose inner nature is an empty writing slate onto which you can inscribe a new context of safety and trust. Now the circle is not vicious any more, and everything you experience contributes to your further evolution.

The alternative to suppression is awareness and understanding. With awareness and understanding, when evolution accelerates, your capacity to include or *be with* that which previously you've been avoiding expands. When you can include what previously you've been resisting, you naturally open up to the greater whole, rather than contract with fear in the face of it. And when you are open in the face of the greater whole, you are able to re-create that which you previously resisted becoming aware of.

Whenever you re-create an incompletion, it will naturally complete itself and disappear. By re-creation I mean letting what is suppressed appear in the clear light of day. So re-creation allows you to have a thorough experience of what you previously resisted. When you resist you get persistence. When you expand to re-create and include, and when you have a thorough experience of what you previously resisted, the suppressed content integrates and disappears. It disappears as stuck energy and integrates into the greater whole.

Prana and the Pineal Gland

The Rebirthing process facilitates all this. I mentioned how oxygen is required to process energy when emotion is excited either externally or internally. Actually there is another aspect to the energy of the breath beyond this ordinary, three-dimensional facilitation of physical and emotional process. This is the aspect of *prana.*

Prana is a special energy that is connected with air and breath. It is like an inner lining to the air we breathe, and it has a special role to play in relation to higher consciousness. When we breathe properly we not only take in ordinary oxygen but we absorb *prana* through a special tube that runs through the center of our body. The prana tube stretches, when you are standing, from one hand's length beneath your feet to one hand's length above your head. If you make a circle with your thumb and middle finger, the diameter of the circle is the tube's diameter. Proper breathing draws *prana* in from both ends of the tube so that it flows through the pineal gland in the center of the head and gathers in our chakras. *Prana* is the energy aspect of multidimensional consciousness, and absorbing it into our chakras and allowing it to pass through our pineal gland is one of the key factors in our experiencing the unity of all life everywhere. *Prana* breathing stopped when Atlantis fell.

Until very recently the pineal gland was treated by biologists as a "vestigial" organ—an organ with no known present function. Present-day biologists have begun to become aware that the pineal gland is light sensitive and that it plays a variety of roles in ordinary physiology. But the pineal gland is far more than even an active physical organ. The awakened pineal gland is like an eye that opens onto higher-dimensional reality. It is our point of contact with the new Christ Consciousness grid that is energizing the planet and leading it towards its rebirth on the fourth dimension. When we breathe through the prana tube and activate the pineal gland, we experience unity; when we don't breathe that way we experience separation; so the direct experience of not breathing that way is separation or polarity consciousness.

The purpose of the breathing practices described in *Nothing* and *Something* was simply to restore our access to *prana,* to reawaken the pineal gland, and to restore higher dimensional awareness.

In the Rebirthing process, when *prana* passes through the pineal gland it acts as an internal cleaning mechanism. With the acceleration of evolution huge amounts of energy are flushing through us all the time, much of it passing into our systems even if we are not prepared to receive it. This influx of energy stimulates the energy stuck in our unconscious, and, if resisted, contributes to emotional instability. But if we are prepared, i.e., if we have created a setting of awareness, understanding, safety and trust so that we are open to what's going on and don't have to close down to it, the *prana* moving through the body brings about a simple displacement process, causing a layer at a time of incompletions from the past to come to consciousness. When this occurs, you may or may not be aware of the content of these incompletions. You may feel the release of energy in the form of crying and grief, exhilaration and joy, anger and rage; or you may pass into a state of hyper-dimensional consciousness, experiencing the expansion of pure energy move in your body and your awareness. Memories of incomplete contents may arise spontaneously: memories of traumatic experiences or episodes from past lives, of the scene of your birth or scenes from your childhood. Or you may recover wishes, desires, ideas, and intentions that you had been harboring unconsciously and not been aware of. Any or all or only a few of these things may occur. The content of these incompletions is less important than the release of the energy behind them. But in any case all you really need to do is stay open so that you can allow yourself to feel it rising and passing through you.

What matters most is that you allow yourself *to stay with* whatever arises and experience each layer thoroughly. The thorough experience of what is activated is the re-creation of the original, suppressed experience. The re-creation of suppressed experience enables that experience to come to a natural completion and finally to utterly disappear and integrate into the greater whole.

When something integrates, you are no longer in opposition to it; or, to put it the other way, when you are no longer in opposition to something, it spontaneously integrates. You've expanded to include it so that now it can contribute to your greater good and to the greater good of all life everywhere.

The essence of Rebirthing is this: by taking in prana directly we flush out the stuck energy of our incompletions from the past, integrating that which we previously had been suppressing. Since suppression is based on Polarity Consciousness—suppressing what we feel is bad and only allowing ourselves to be aware of what we think of as good—the Rebirthing process automatically takes us from polarity to unity. We no longer are making judgements about the stuff that is inside us—we let it all come out—good or bad, pleasant or unpleasant—so that it can integrate and disappear into the greater whole.

The fact that in Rebirthing we let it all come out should

put us on the alert that, unlike many "New Age" weekend workshops, Rebirthing is not a temporary "high." A weekend of Rebirthing is something quite different from processes that may very well help you experience states of mind that are quite positive in themselves but where a few days or a few weeks after the workshop is over you are right back where you started from or worse—where you are left in a depression because you have lost what you thought you had gained, and no idea how to regain what you've lost. What comes up in Rebirthing may be positive or negative. It may be painful or joyous, fascinating or terrifying. What you actually experience, one way or the other—is only half the story. The other half is the fact that in undergoing the Rebirthing process you have changed the very context of your experience from polarity to unity, and are thereby prepared to work with whatever is inside you no matter what it happens to be.

Part III

No Time Like the Present

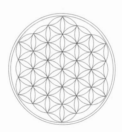

The Fall of Atlantis

We are coming to the end of an immense period of history. The present epoch of human life on Earth began 13,000 years ago when the magnetic and gravitational poles shifted and the continent of Atlantis fell into the sea. It was a finále a to a series of problems that had actually begun 3,000 years before, when an enormous comet crashed into the Earth at the place where Charleston South Carolina is today.

The problems were caused by the Martians who had been living among us on Atlantis for over 50,000 years, more or less peacefully, but after the comet struck, co-existence between the two races—humans and Martians—was no longer possible.

The Martians came to Atlantis uninvited during the early days of Atlantean history (about 65,000 years ago), and established themselves as a separate and sometimes dissonant minority among the Atlantean population. The Martians had highly over-developed left brains, and virtually no right brains. They were thus capable of enormous feats of intellectual and technical mastery—they knew how to create and operate the external Merkaba and had in fact come to Atlantis by this means. But the Martians were completely underdeveloped emotionally and intuitively. The rest of the Atlanteans, by contrast, were highly developed intuitively, and were very reluctant to interfere with the course of history by purely external technological means. Conflicts had arisen between the Martians and the rest of the Atlanteans throughout their long history, but now that the continent was known to be threatened by an approaching comet, two unreconcilable approaches to the danger emerged. The Martians wanted to use technology to blast the comet out of the sky. The humans wanted to accept the catastrophe as an act of God. The human majority won the day, and the comet was allowed to crash into Earth, but it landed precisely on the part of the continent inhabited by the Martians. From that moment on the Martians refused to go on with the charade of cooperating with the humans. They determined to deploy the external Merkaba by which they had come to Earth in the first place, and to attempt to gain control over the Earth and its unreliable human inhabitants.

What they only succeeded in doing was wreaking havoc with the dimensional system of the planet itself, resulting in a rip in the energy field of the Earth that sucked in an influx of lower forms of beings from other dimensional realities, complicating and confusing spiritual life on Earth. When the gravitational and magnetic pole shifts occurred and the dimensional level of the planet plummeted to the third-dimensional level, the disturbances created by the Martian catastrophe simply continued in another form. The human-Martian conflict is one of the incompletions from our past that we have carried with us for the past 13,000 years.

The Precession of the Equinoxes

Though from the point of view of the kind of consciousness that we possess today all this looks like a series of historical misfortunes, there is a deeper truth to this history. Historical time on the scale that we are talking about is governed by vast astronomical / astrological cycles. These in turn orchestrate and organize the evolution of the consciousness of the planet. The events on Atlantis correspond precisely to the movement of these cosmic patterns.

What is popularly referred to as the Aquarian Age—the period of history that we are presently moving into—also has to do with these same cosmic cycles. The cycle in question is called the precession of the equinoxes. The "equinoxes" are the points on the annual calendar when night and day are equal. At the present time the equinoxes occur on approximately March 21 and September 21, the first days of spring and autumn (in the Northern Hemisphere) of every year. If you are familiar with astrology, you know that these points correspond to the beginning of the signs Aries in March and Libra in September. What does this mean astronomically? Well, the astrological signs are constellations along a band of the sky called the "ecliptic." The planets as well as the sun and moon appear to move along this band. When an astrologer says that the planet Mercury is "in" the sign of Virgo, for instance, he means that the constellation Virgo is the background against which Mercury at present appears. Though you can't actually see the sign during the day, the sun also stands out against the background of the ecliptic. When we say that March 21 is the beginning of the sign of Aries, you would think that this means that the constellation behind the sun on that date would be Aries. In actual fact this not the case. This is where the precession of the equinoxes comes in. Owing to a tilt in the Earth's axis, the precise position of the sun against the ecliptic appears to change approximately one astrological sign every 2,160 years or so. At the time when the astrological system in use today was first put into writing, the sun was indeed "in" Aries; but for the last 2,000 years it has actually been in the sign of Pisces, and, at the present time, it is about to pass into the sign of Aquarius—hence the term for the New Age—the "Aquarian Age."

Now it takes about 25,920 years for the precession of the equinoxes to complete a cycle, i.e., for the equinoxes to "pre-

cess" or move backward through all twelve signs of the
Zodiac. It is this vast cycle, sometimes called a "Great Year,"
that controls the basic characteristics of the historical periods. Cultural patterns and values change with the change in
signs. The cycle as a whole orchestrates a pulsation in the
level of consciousness of the planet. During one half of the
cycle, awareness / consciousness expands. During the other
half it diminishes.

There are two points in the Great Year where the changes
that occur are much greater than changes in cultural values
and ordinary historical transformations. At these points the
Earth undergoes vast energetic transformations, and shifts
in dimensional level can occur. The evolution of the planet
itself happens on this scale, and these two special points are
crisis points at which the major evolutionary shifts are implemented. The two special points in this cycle are situated just
preceding the midway point and just before the beginning
of a new cycle. Since the whole cycle of the Great Year takes
25,920 years, you can see the significance of the fact that the
fall of Atlantis occurred 13,000 years ago. The Atlantean catastrophe occurred precisely at the crisis point in this cycle
where consciousness had reached a point of maximum awak-
eness. After the fall, the planetary mind and the human inhabitants that were its carriers began to plummet. Today, we
have reached the nadir, the very darkest point, and are at
the point where awareness is beginning to return.

Earth Changes

The crisis points are generally accompanied by cataclysmic
changes in the physical condition of the Earth. There are
changes in the Earth's gravitational axis as well as a shift in
its magnetic field. The gravitational changes produce ice ages,
floods, earthquakes, and other geological disruptions. The

magnetic changes produce major alterations in emotional and conscious life. The Earth's magnetic field is connected to human emotion and to our short term memory, for instance.

For the last several hundred years, scientists tell us the strength of the Earth's magnetic field has been in flux, and at present it seems to be decidedly weakening. It is actually possible for all of us to notice this in our own experience. I sure do. For instance, this morning I was holding a tape cassette to make a tape recording. I walked into the kitchen to get a glass of water. I came back to the living room but where was the tape? I knew where it had been just a few minutes before, but where was it now? I experience that sort of thing all the time. Or I walk into the kitchen, and when I get there, I can't remember what I went in there for. I had a perfectly clear game plan, but what happened to it? Well, it could be I'm just getting senile, but I don't think so. It is much more likely that it is the magnetic field and its relation to memory.

The Earth's magnetic field also affects emotional stability. What appears as a break down in family life, as violence among school children, and as epidemic psychopathologies of all kinds, may simply have to do with the fact that the Earth's magnetic field is weakening and that the factor that connected us emotionally to each other through our co-presence in this field, is far less active.

We know that on the third dimensional level our consciousness is physically linked to the electromagnetic nature of our nervous system and to the way our connective tissue, right down to the nuclei of the cells, is a vast web of electromagnetic energies. The interconnection between us and the Earth itself is profoundly one of electromagnetic linkages. So changes in the magnetic field of the Earth effect changes in our relations with each other and with the way we process our feelings.

At the crisis point—the point where the maximum change in dimensional level is possible—what happens is that the magnetic field of the planet actually goes to zero. No magnetic field. At that point we are susceptible to enormous changes in our emotional nature and in our relations to each other, and, unless we have become conscious of our own Merkaba energy vehicles that act as protection fields, our memories are destroyed. This is basically what happened to most of us on Atlantis. Not only was memory erased, but we were thrown down the dimensional lattice, into a dense dark world.

The apparently negative character of what happened to us when Atlantis fell was due to the fact that at the time that the Earth's magnetic field collapsed, we were approaching the highest point—the point of maximum consciousness— in the precession of the equinoxes cycle. When the Earth's magnetic field collapses at the opposite end of the cycle— the point approaching the point of greatest darkness—the collapse can have extraordinarily positive meaning. It can be the site of a great transition from one dimensional level to another higher one. That is precisely what all the prophecies anticipate as happening at the present juncture. When the magnetic field goes to absolute zero, there is a three day period of black-out, and, when the days are passed, the Earth emerges on a higher dimension. That means that the time of greatest crisis, of possible calamities and catastrophes, is also the time of the greatest opportunities.

What Happened When Atlantis Fell

What exactly happened when Atlantis fell? What in particularly did we, as the human species lose?

First of all, if it's true that in our true spiritual form we've been around forever and that we'll continue to be around forever, that means that we've gone through many lifetimes— not only on the planet Earth, and not only in a place where the dominant dimension of consciousness is the third dimension. We have existed on many different dimensional levels, on many different planets. But since the time of Atlantis, the human beings that were part of that civilization have for the most part been reborn again and again on the planet Earth and have therefore participated in the evolution and history of this planet. That means that along with the planet, we fell from the fourth dimension to the third, and that at the same time we passed from the first level of consciousness to the second. What we lost was a level of awareness where we had a much fuller understanding of who we are and where we had a much clearer picture of what was available to us than we do now. As I have mentioned repeatedly, in Atlantis we experienced reality from the perspective of the Unity of Being, not the point of view of polarity and separation that we experience now. Materially, we had awareness of a much greater range of the electromagnetic spectrum, not just the narrow bands of light and sound that we are aware of now. Dolphins, for example, are able to perceive a much greater range than we are. Much of what's happening even in the physical world just passes us by. That hasn't always been the case. We've had a much greater range of perception and consequently a much greater range of understanding than what we have right now.

Apart from awareness of a wider spectral range, on most higher-dimensional levels we have awareness of our multidimensional nature, all of which is cut off to us here. It is as if when Atlantis fell we went to sleep and forgot who we are. Veil upon veil of slumber were made to cover our consciousness. But these veils are actually necessary for our well-being here. If we had full awareness of our multi-dimensional nature but were unable to change the dimensional level of the world around us, life would be too painful for us to go on. But it had to go on. This world, in which we experience the Second Level of Consciousness, is a stepping stone to a higher level of consciousness. It is a bridge that we have to cross in order for the planetary level to evolve. The time has now arrived for us to awaken in order to usher in that new level. Slowly but surely we are awakening to the memory of who we were and to the higher reality of what we are.

When Atlantis crashed, the change in level of consciousness occurred not only in terms of human experience, but it happened for the entire Earth. What caused this change was that the grid of Christ Consciousness that surrounded the Earth and was responsible for sustaining the level of human consciousness was destroyed.

A grid is necessary for any species to exist. There is a grid for every form of life on the planet, without which that form of life would not exist. Any time a species becomes extinct— as in fact more than half of them on this planet have by now —what happens is that its grid dissolves. It just disappears. This happened when Atlantis fell in regard to the human grid, and it was immediately replaced by a different one of an entirely different character. The kind of consciousness that is associated with a grid is determined by Sacred Geometry. The grid that replaced the grid for the first level of consciousness and that we've had for the past 13,000 years is a totally masculine grid based, on squares and triangles. It is dominated by left-brain consciousness. Actually the grid for Christ Consciousness—the third level—was there in Atlantis, but it was destroyed as a result of the fall. Today there are three grids: the ones for the first and second levels, and the recently completed *new* Christ Consciousness grid. When the next shift happens, the first and second grids will disappear.

Thoth and the Ascended Masters on Atlantis were aware that Atlantis was going to fall. For 16,000 years Thoth—under the name of Chiquetet Arlich Vomalites—had been King of Atlantis. 200 years before the fall he knew exactly what was going to happen, so he along with two other Ascended Masters—Ra and Araaragot—got permission to create a new grid synthetically. They assembled what you might call the "blueprint" for a new Christ Consciousness grid, and initiated the process of preparing it for the time, some 13,000 years in the future, when it once again would be the grid for the human species on the planet. They went to Egypt, which at the time was known as Khem, and they began by digging a shaft in the ground a mile deep, connecting to the axis point for the Christ Consciousness grid.

The new grid itself is a geometrical fishnet-like electromagnetic structure and it is this that is allowing the new consciousness to come forth. It sits roughly sixty miles above the Earth. Its structure is a relationship between a dodecahedron and an icosohedron. Both figures are based on pentagons. Now an icosohedron is a "stellated," i.e. "starred" pentagon. Five little tetrahedrons fit perfectly into the side of a pentagon to form an icosohedronal cap, a kind of point that together makes it look like a star. If you stellate all twelve sides of a dodecahedron, you have exactly what the new grid looks like. The stellated dodecahedron is considered to be feminine in character, so the new grid will allow our feminine, right-brained, intuitive component to come forth.

Besides initiating the new Christ Consciousness grid, Thoth activated a Merkaba field in order to protect the Earth from the pole shifts ahead. First Thoth and the others built three pyramids based on the spiraling energy arising from the axis point of the grid. These three pyramids include the one that we know today as the "Great Pyramid" and the two others that sit nearby it. This was all in preparation, as I say, for what they knew would happen 200 years later when the poles would shift and the dimensions fall.

What they used The Great Pyramid for at that time was this. It served as a platform for a curious kind of spaceship that usually sits a mile beneath the Earth, beneath the sphinx. This spaceship is only three to five atoms thick, and it resides most of the time in a dimension one overtone higher than whatever the Earth is on. Because of this slight dimensional discrepancy, it can pass right through the Earth. As the magnetic field of the Earth was going into the last stages of collapse, they took that ship and moved it from its place beneath the Earth and went to Atlantis as it was being inundated. They picked up the Ascended Masters, and Thoth says that they got no more than a quarter of a mile off the ground when Undal, the last island to remain above water, sank into the sea. Then they brought the ship to a special landing platform on top of the Great Pyramid as the magnetic field continued to degenerate. The final collapse of the field took three-and-a-half days. When it finally went to zero all human memory went with it. The only way to avoid this memory loss during the field collapse is if you have mastery of the Merkaba. You can then create your own magnetic field from its counter-rotating fields of light and thus retain your memory. The Ascended Masters on top of the Pyramid formed a huge Merkaba energy field and remained within it for the three-and-a-half days. When this period was over they emerged into a whole new world—the world of the third dimension.

The Legacy of 1972

What is happening in the world today is a product both of the precise point where we are in time in terms of the precession of the equinoxes, and the fact that the Christ Consciousness grid is now fully matured and ready to be put into

action. But these cosmic facts are completely reflected in our
state of consciousness; and in fact you could say they *are* our
state of consciousness. Whatever is happening in the external world is a reflection of what is happening inside us, individually and collectively. The process is not a "linear" one:
it doesn't happen like a simple chain of causes and effects.
You certainly can't say that we are *causing* the precession of
the equinoxes, nor can you say that our position in the vast
cosmic cycle is the simple, linear cause of the fact that we are
on the verge of awakening to a new level of consciousness.
These are two aspects of the same event: the transformation
of the consciousness of the Earth and the transformation of
the consciousness of the individuals on the Earth are two
aspects of one reality that are mutually and reciprocally inter-
connected. And yet, it is true that we are at the point in time
where the entire Earth is supposed to be ready to ascend to
the fourth dimension, and we are about to complete our passage across the bridge of the second level of consciousness
and enter the third. And there have been many prophecies,
both by tribal peoples around the world—and by gifted seers
from our own culture—that have predicted this, and seen
that the time for this great spiritual awakening to occur is
our time. In fact, by most accounts the ascension should already have happened. The prophecies also have foretold that
there would be great changes in the geography of the Earth,
as one would expect from the precession phenomena. But
the catastrophes have not happened. And we are still here.
So what is going on?

Well, there are certain other events on a cosmic scale that
have changed things drastically and created a situation on
Earth at the present time that is actually unique in the history of our galaxy. So much so, that neither the Melchizedeks
nor the Ascended Masters are quite certain about what is
happening! Thoth believed that it was possible that we were

going to be able to ascend together all at once and not have to pass through the catastrophic Earth changes that usually attend ascension.

The main unexpected event occurred on August 7, 1972 when an eruption of titanic proportions occurred on the sun. If you look it up in the newspapers from that time, you will see that astrophysicists were reporting enormous solar winds of up to 2½ million miles an hour. These lasted for three days and then subsided to 1½ million for thirty days. As a matter of fact what the scientists picked up was just a small part of what really occurred. What actually happened was that the sun changed its internal physical constitution and expanded way out into the solar system—actually as far as Jupiter— and it would have destroyed the Earth had it not been for the intervention of the Sirians.

The Sirians

Sirius is the star in the northern sky that is closest to our solar system. It is the brightest star in the sky, located to the left and straight down from the belt of Orion and can be seen with the naked eye on most nights of the year. It has certain remarkable astronomical properties. It has a companion star, "Sirius B." The two stars circle around each other and this double-star system is linked intimately with our own solar system. In fact we travel about the galaxy together with Sirius.

But Sirius is interesting for much more important reasons than mere astronomical curiosity. The whole story about Sirius and who the inhabitants of Sirius are was told fully in *Nothing*. The information there comes from the writings of Zacharia Sitchin, particularly *The Twelfth Planet* and *Genesis Revisited*. But I will recapitulate the story briefly here so you can understand why the Sirians have taken such a decisive interest in our destiny. It has to do with who and what the human race is and begins in the far distant past.

The tenth planet in our solar system (which Sitchin refers to as the twelfth planet) and which is unknown to conventional astronomy at the present time, is called Nibiru. It has a long, elliptical orbit, and travels in the opposite direction from the rest of the planets. Its celestial journey passes way out beyond the sun and then cuts in between Mars and Jupiter every 3,600 years. Sitchin says that about 450,000 years ago Nibiru and its inhabitants, the Nefilim, experienced a problem with its atmosphere that resulted in its inability to retain heat. Since for long parts of their orbit they were extremely far from the sun, even under normal circumstances the sun could not be its source of heat. Heat came from the inside of the planet. The problem was retaining the heat the planet generated. Nibiru needed to have what today we call the "green-house effect"—it had to use its atmosphere to lock in heat and prevent it from escaping into outer space. At this time, however, the planet was losing its heat via some sort of a hole in the atmosphere—no doubt something like the hole in our "ozone layer" that ecologists are so exercised about. The Nefilim discovered that gold dust suspended in the atmosphere was the solution to their problem and that Earth was a good source of gold. So they came here to mine it, and for 200,000 years they survived by doing that. Whenever, in its 3,600 year orbit, Nibiru came close enough to Earth, they picked up vast loads of gold and brought them home and place them in their atmosphere. But after 200,000 years, the Nefilim, who had been living on the Earth as laborers serving the home planet for all that time, got tired of their labors and rebelled. The Nefilim then decided to create a race of subservient beings who would be nothing but slaves dedicated to the mining of gold. That subservient race turned out to be us!

At this point in Sitchin's narrative, Thoth himself, according to Drunvalo, added some crucial corrective information regarding exactly how the production of the human race was accomplished. The Nefilim served as the "Mother" aspect of the new species. But they required a complementary "Father" aspect to complete the task. This is where the Sirians come in.

The Sirians already had a connection to our solar system. As I mentioned, they are in a sense our traveling companions on our journey about the galaxy. (It is from this connection, by the way, that our true relations to the dolphins is derived. The third planet out from Sirius B is mainly a water planet, and the bulk of the civilization is cetacean— whale-like creatures, as are the dolphins. Dolphins actually travel interdimensionally from here to there and there to here on a daily basis.)

The Sirians, having this connection with Earth, became our father aspect. Thoth says that a family of thirty-two of them came from Sirius B and went to the Halls of Amenti. The Halls of Amenti are a mysterious womb-like dimensional warp created more than 5½ million years ago and existing today 1,000 miles inside the Earth. Before the Sirians arrived, seven Nefilim had dropped their bodies, forming seven spheres of consciousness, and had merged into the pattern from Sacred Geometry known as the Seed of Life *(figure 3.1)* to create an ovum, causing a special flame to appear: a cool, blue-white light in the form of a flame but without heat, four feet high. The flame was placed into the Halls of Amenti, and when the Sirians arrived they merged with the flame. (The Flame of Life, and the Seed of Life are described in great detail in *Nothing.*) The period of the gestation process was 2000 years. So 2000 years later we started coming out. This was about 200,000 years ago.

Because they functioned as our Father aspect, the Sirians have a paternal concern for our well being, and it is because

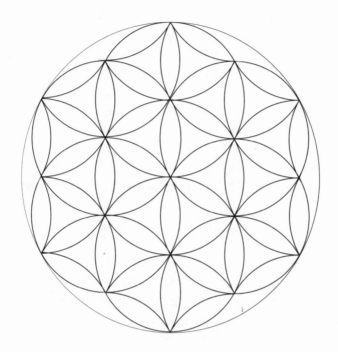

Figure 3–1. The Seed of Life.

of this that they undertook to intervene when, in 1972, we were threatened by the solar pulse.

The Sirians undertook this intervention with complete permission from the higher centers in the hierarchy of Being. It must be understood that if they had not done so everyone and everything—every last bug on the planet—would have been completely wiped out. No third-dimensional planet can survive being inside the sun. But a fourth-dimensional planet would not experience any problem at all. The inhabitant of a planet on the higher overtones of the fourth dimension would simply be able to tune in to the physical changes that absorption by the solar pulse would have caused, acclimate themselves to them, and simply go on existing without interruption.

But we and our planet were still on the third dimension and would have been completely wiped out. And it seems that the planet Earth figures in some as yet unrevealed plans of the hierarchy of Being itself, so the Sirians were able to get permission from higher galactic levels to save us. They did this by inserting a holographic protection field around us, around the planet, so it would seem that we had entered into a parallel universe in which the only thing that seemed to have happened was what our astrophysicists recorded, enormously powerful solar winds, but nothing more consequential.

The Holographic Protection Field

That holographic protection field is still there, still protecting us. When it was first put up in 1972 the Sirians retained complete control of it, but they have slowly relinquished that control so that right now it is in our power. How these things play out—what sort of possibilities will be realized—is now entirely up to us.

There are three aspects to the circumstance of the Sirians' inserting this field that we need to understand. First, they couldn't do it without "permission." This was no rogue operation. It wasn't like, for instance, the various escapades of the Martians who first destroyed life on their own planet, then escaped to Atlantis, and finally brought about the dimensional catastrophes connected to the fall of Atlantis by using, *without* permission, external Merkaba technology in an attempt to save their necks. The Sirians were working, as I say, with full knowledge and permission of the "higher-ups" in the cosmic hierarchy.

Second, the insertion of the field had to be accomplished without our being aware either of the imminence of the danger or of the solution.

Third, at the same time that they saved us, the Sirians had

to create conditions that would speed up our own evolution so that we would be able to enter the fourth dimension and from that perspective be able to protect ourselves.

You can see how fate, accident, and our own inner spiritual work combine to accomplish destiny in some mysterious way that we cannot understand from our third-dimensional perspective. According to the cosmic calendar exemplified by the precession of equinoxes, about this time (in the winter of 1998) we were due to progress to the third level of consciousness and enter the fourth dimension. But it was clear that as a species we were very far from having reached such a level. In order to be on schedule, some how or other our growth would have to be accelerated. And it seems that the anomaly of the solar pulse of 1972 created just the conditions that would lead to such an acceleration.

Well, the process of acceleration has indeed occurred. And not only that, it is going on at an unprecedented rate. Things are changing at such a pace that we have attracted the attention of the entire galaxy! What is going on on Earth today is something that no one anywhere in this region of the universe has ever seen or heard of before—at least the Ascended Masters and Melchizedeks have never known of it before. And the acceleration isn't stopping. What the Masters and Melchizedeks do know is that whatever happens here is not only going to be unique; it's going to have a unique impact on all life everywhere.

It's almost as though the plug has been pulled and an enormous flood of consciousness has been released, or that seeds have been planted in great abundance, with incredible consequences for new growths of being throughout the galaxy.

Everybody knows today that the last twenty-five years or so have seen an incredible acceleration of technological, historical, and social changes across the entire planet: the end of the Cold War, the coming of a global economy, the en-

trance into the "information age" with a computer in every
living room and a cell phone in every jacket pocket. These
changes have created enormous disruptions in human life,
from terrible increases in emotional and psychological turmoil, to the break down of families, to the disruption of traditional cultures everywhere. This much is known to everybody. But these changes are just the tip of the iceberg. What
has been actually going on at an internal level will have consequences going far beyond the mere disruption of personal
lives, economies, and cultures.

To see how and why this is happening you have to look
at just what was entailed by the implementation of the "solution" to the solar-pulse crisis that the Sirians came up with.
In 1972, when they first looked into the Akashic Record for
a solution to the kind of problem that we were facing, they
saw that there had never been a solution. If a star erupted
on the third dimension, the third dimensional planets in orbit
about it and within the compass of its explosion were simply consumed by the expansion. But then they looked further to see if anybody had even *thought* of a possible solution,
even if it hadn't been implemented. And what they found
was that the idea of accelerating the evolution of a planet so
it could handle events that would otherwise be disastrous
had indeed been thought of. The concept was on record but
it had never been tried. And so this is what they tried.

By the way, this process of checking the great cosmic memory bank—the Akashic Record—not only for what has been
tried, but for possibilities that had merely been proposed—
is itself instructive. It shows how every thought, every intuition of a possibility—even if it is only an idea, even if there
are no present means or conditions for its implementation—
is extremely important and remains a part of the greater reality. Reality includes not only *facts* but *possibilities.* You could
say that it's as though somebody had planted a seed, or even

that God had planted the seed. Somewhere at some time in some galaxy, on some dimension or other, who knows where, the concept of accelerating the evolution of a planet in order to change its material fate, was conceived of, in full knowledge that at some point it would be implemented, and that when that seed was planted and used, it would bring forth a whole new possibility, a whole new way that life would develop itself. And that seems to be what's happening here.

The Lucifer Experiment

I want to point out that the technology involved in the production of the holographic protection field was a highly developed form of technology. It was not, for instance, an internal Merkaba field. The Earth's Merkaba field has in fact awakened, but that is an entirely different matter. The holographic protection field is ordinary, Luciferian technology, and yet the fact that it has been inserted around the Earth at this time seems to be allowing a whole new possibility to come forth — a possibility that may have consequences and significance on a scale that goes far beyond the mere fate of this planet.

One can say that if a possibility exists, somewhere, some time, some how, life is going to try it. In this sense the universe itself is a vast experimental laboratory in which possibility after possibility is explored, and the significance of each one for the manifestation of Unity of Being is examined.

The new possibility being tried out right now may involve the resolution of the age-old conflict between internal and external technology, which is itself a reflection of the war between Lucifer and Michael that has been going on since time immemorial. There were three Lucifer "rebellions" prior to the present, each one ending with the entire solar system in total chaos and disaster. And so far it has looked as if this fourth experiment was going to end up the same way. But there is a new possibility now.

I told the whole story of the Lucifer rebellions in *Nothing*. I am not going to repeat it in too much detail here, but, in brief, Lucifer was a great archangel—the most magnificent of all the angels. His name means "Bearer of Light" or "The Bright and Shining One." It is actually better to see what Lucifer did, not as a *rebellion,* but rather as an *experiment.* The experiment was to create free will. Prior to this experiment everything that happened in the universe happened entirely according to divine plan. There was no deviation from it; nothing occurred according to chance; there was no manifestation of things imagined but yet unrealized. The possibility of freedom, of newness, of spontaneity, of free imagination, had not yet been tried.

The way this new possibility emerged had everything to do with who Lucifer was and where he was in the cosmic hierarchy. Lucifer was the highest being in all creation with the exception of God the creator. Now, when you look at how we ourselves are motivated to act, you can see that it is completely normal for us to aspire to be or to be like whatever we take to be better or higher than we are. We want to *become* what we *admire.* But for Lucifer, there was no one except the Creator who was higher on the absolute scale of value than Lucifer himself. So there was no ambition, no aspiration, available to him except to imitate God. Well and good. But when we aspire to some form of excellence, we often wish not only to equal our hero but to go him one better! If we are an Olympic runner, we want to beat the record for the fifty-yard dash, not just to equal it. And this was true of Lucifer. He wanted to go one better than God. And not only that—his desire to do this came with God's blessings.

Now the paramount achievement of God was clearly the creation of the world. And it was no secret how God had in fact done this: the world had been created by an *internal* process in which the figures from Sacred Geometry were taken as *patterns,* and the world and the things of this world were produced by *imagining* the world into existence according to these patterns. There was a kind of continuity, or flow, or, if you like, a love-link between Creator and Creation, because everything that was created flowed directly from the Creator's being. The other archangels—Michael, Gabriel, and so forth—remained within the love-link. Their way of getting about in the world was through a "light body" and through the continuous expression of their harmonious alignment with the Creator. And it seems that for most of life in the universe, the way things happen, they way things are done, is through the light body. The dolphins for instance live this way. They have nothing outside of themselves. They have everything they need via their internal Merkaba fields. They can do anything they want without experiencing conflicts among themselves. They don't need technology at all.

But Lucifer wished to create in a way that was different from God's way. To do this he had to separate from God's love, from his creativity. In short, what he did was invent left-brain technology: a way of creating things and making things happen by cold objective logic and the manipulation of material reality according to laws that had nothing whatever to do with inner being. He exploited dualism and Polarity Consciousness to find a new way of creating. And he created beings who, like himself, were wholly dominated by this way of being. These beings were the Greys and the Martians, whom I wrote about in *Nothing,* as well as certain types of humans who are completely addicted to material technological thinking.

The result is that the world has been torn apart by a war between Michael and Lucifer, between the forces of light and darkness, between love and inner wisdom on the one hand and technology and willfulness on the other. This war is of great moment to us. Much of the history of the past

13,000 years can be read as various chapters in the struggle between these two forces or tendencies. And the reason that this has been so is that the human being him or herself shares in them both.

Though today we human beings seem more and more dominated by our own technology, we retain at our core a spark of love. We have the possibility of discovering our light bodies, of awakening our internal Merkaba fields, of experiencing our inner link with divine creative energy. We are not only intellects. We are hearts and imaginations. We can live not only according to Factuality, but according to Possibility. Up until now, this division in our being has been a reflection of the war between Michael and Lucifer. What conventional religion refers to as our "souls" have been the battleground for this entirely dualistic process. This is what our conventional religious ideas of good and evil tell us. But it is precisely this dualistic process that seems now to be coming to an end. Because we have both a core of love and a left-brain intelligence, the possibility is there that we might merge these two ways of being and produce a kind of life never seen before, one that will ultimately resolve this age-old conflict.

If this is to happen it will involve combining an internal connection with our light bodies and the *permitted* application of external technology: external technology that is utilized without the dualism and internal separation that external technology usually implies. And this possibility seems to be in part the result of the Sirian experiment with the holographic protection field placed around the Earth in 1972 to save us from the solar pulse. It was an exercise in external technology that is having the effect of speeding up our evolution, so that we can enter the fourth dimension, bring about the ascension of the entire planet, and consummate the awakening that our position in the 13,000 year equinoctial cycle indicates we are ready for.

Right-Brain Technology

But how exactly are we to understand the relation between left-brain, Luciferian technology, and the new utilization of technology that is going to bring about all these changes? Drunvalo himself went through a quandary about this, and in a way his story is almost a parable about how the whole race is going to learn to get beyond the conflict between external technology on the one hand and the self-sufficiency of the light body on the other.

At a certain point Drunvalo had gone way down the road of technology: he began using external technological means to experiment with states of consciousness. He found he was able to do incredible things, like jump-starting people's Merkaba fields to help them travel into extra-dimensional worlds. He accomplished this electronically by stimulating human energy fields and causing them to interact with electrical fields at certain frequencies. It was no different from the external Merkaba that the Martians had employed, or the Philadelphia experiment and the Montauk project. But at a certain point Drunvalo's angels came to him and in essence reminded him that they had warned him about going down the road of external technology years before; and they reminded him about the eternal battle between Lucifer and the archangel Michael, and about the possibility of activating one's own energy field internally, as the dolphins had done and the whales had done, and how these creatures required nothing outside of themselves; that they didn't have to monkey around with the external Merkaba or utilize all this external mechanical gadgetry.

They pointed out how every time you use machinery to achieve some desired end you give your power away. If you are sitting in a cold room, you can heat the room with an electric heater. It will warm you up, but if it does, you will have no incentive to discover how to warm yourself from within. The Tibetans know very well how to generate an internal heat that will allow them to survive Himalayan winters comfortably without garments. But if you use a heater, you will never discover how they do it. You will have given away your own potential power to the heating device. The further you go down that road, the more powerless and dependent you become. What is true of generating heat is even more fatefully true of jump-starting one's Merkaba field, so they recommended very strongly not going down the road of external technology.

Drunvalo was chastened. He abandoned external technology. He gave away his equipment. He became a veritable Luddite, thinking that the angels meant him to reject all technological assistance of every kind whatsoever. But a few years later, the angels came again, and said, you have gone a little too far. There is another possibility that you haven't considered. And they recommended that he reflect this time on the Sirians, our Father aspect, who had discovered another kind of technology altogether—a right-brain technology—a technology that did not reject the use of technical equipment, but on the contrary, put it to an altogether extraordinary use. With right-brain technology, the angels told him, you can do anything that you can do with left brain technology, but you don't throw away your inner power by doing so. The idea is that you have to *link* with the technology, so that it becomes an *extension* of yourself, rather than something outside of yourself. A dowsing rod is a good example of a right-brain technological device. The dowser uses a forked piece of wood to help him find water. But he does so by becoming one with it. All the technology that we have can be treated that way. You align yourself with the internal sense of what the technology is trying to accomplish, and eventually you will not need the technology at all. You enlist the intuitive side of the brain, the right brain, and recover the power that the left brain had surrendered to the machine.

The angels said the Sirians were using right brain technology right now to step out of the conditions created by the Luciferian rebellion. With right-brain technology you can learn for yourself what the technology is showing you, and you can get to the point where you can do without the technology. So the equipment is a bridge. And they said that's the way out. It would be very difficult for us to give all of our technology away in a day. It would be like asking ourselves to take off all our clothes and go into the forest and learn how to survive naked. Well, good luck! So we need a bridge, and the bridge is right-brain technology.

The Kogi

There is a bit more to say about the pulse from the sun. Though it would have destroyed all life on the planet if the Sirians had not constructed the holographic protection field, there are qualities of this light that are very positive. From the time of the pulse in 1972 until some time in 1995, these positive influences were held at bay by the protection field, but since 1995 they have been allowed to enter Earth-space and the Earth itself, and are part of the picture of how the transformation of consciousness on Earth is taking place.

Incidentally, the priests of the Japanese Shinto religion have been aware that a new kind of light from the sun would one day emerge and transform life on Earth. They associated this light with their sun-goddess, Amaterasu, and they say that for 500 years this light has been hidden, but it is now emerging and allowing a feminine form of life to re-emerge. The Mayans, who are themselves survivors from Atlantis, are also aware of the coming of a new kind of light from the sun.

Drunvalo has been working for some time with a surviving group of the ancient Mayans in the jungles of Guatemala. His work with them has involved collaboration with a Mayan shaman named Hunbatz Men. What they have been doing is working to stabilize this new light from the sun and to integrate it so that it can contribute to the emergence of fourth-dimensional consciousness. About two years ago an associate of Hunbatz Men approached Drunvalo and informed him about a tribal people living in a remote jungle in Columbia.

You might have seen, some time ago, a film on public television made by the BBC about a remote Columbian tribe that lived until that time in apparently complete seclusion, without contact with the so-called civilized world. The film was titled "From the Heart of the World—The Elder Brothers' Warning." This tribe—the Kogi—had allowed the filmmakers to visit and film them because they wanted to send us a message. They said that their sacred mountain, which they referred to as "The Heart of the World," was "dying" and that if it did die, the whole world would die too. Apparently meteorological changes brought about by modern man's contamination of the environment had created a drought at The Heart of the World and a disastrous dearth of snowfall, and if these conditions continued, they saw that the life of the Earth itself was endangered. They said that this was their first and only warning to us, and that they would not contact us again.

Recently, however, they seem to have changed their mind and they have made contact with Drunvalo. He has learned a lot more about the Kogi and how his work is in a sense profoundly linked to their view of things.

The Kogi have no word-language in our sense. They communicate telepathically through little sounds that they make which are not words. These sounds are not, like civilized speech, based on a code. In our speech, word-sounds with more or less fixed meanings are combined to represent ideas about the world. The Kogi's communication through sound goes back to something much more profound and ancient that probably underlies our speech too but, like so many other civilized developments, has been covered over and lost because of the very advantageous things these developments bring. The sounds the Kogi make are tiny, articulate "heart sounds"—little noises rising spontaneously from the heart. When uttered or when heard, they conjure up internal images —the same images in the minds of the person uttering them and the person hearing them. They seem to be sounds from the Dream Time, the plane of being that all people share internally but which is covered over by conscious life, or, another way of putting this, is unperceivable on the second level of consciousness.

The Kogi also retain the use of their light bodies and are able to travel about the face of the Earth without physically leaving their jungle seclusion. They have actually been monitoring what has been happening on Earth but had never before attempted to communicate with us. But since their awareness of the danger to The Heart of the World, their sacred mountain, they decided dire measures were necessary. What they saw is that we humans are not merely unaware, unconscious, or asleep. They think we are actually dead! They say that the life force in the "dream" that we have generated around us to live in is so weak that we are only a spectral shadow of what we might be; that, in effect, we are so dim that we are barely real, and that, through the gross misuse of our own consciousness, we are about to draw the entire world into our shadowy existence.

The Kogi anticipated that on August 11,1999, the date of an important solar eclipse, we would simply fade away into our own feeble dream, taking our weakly imagined world along with us. Only they and the Mayans—whom they had perceived had retained their light bodies too—would survive. But August 11th came and went and we were still here. When they looked again to see if anything had changed, they perceived that indeed something had: that all around the world there were people who had awakened to their Light Bodies, and that we had generated enough life-force in our collective "dream," not exactly to sustain the old world's existence, but to produce a *parallel reality*—one in which the disaster inevitable in the old world would not occur. Because they also saw that it was in part through Drunvalo's instructions in awakening the internal Merkaba that this miracle had occurred, they began to contact Drunvalo, and he is in fact learning to speak their "heart sound" language with instructions to teach it to us.

Many Parallel Worlds

So it seems that it is possible that what not only the Kogi but many other prophets have divined, has actually already occurred! The poles may have shifted, and the Earth may be lying in ruins either from dire geophysical catastrophes or as a result of human technological arrogance and folly. It is possible that this has occurred but that we are no longer living in the world where it happened. This may sound very strange, no doubt, but we may have shifted onto a parallel reality—a reality parallel the one that was prophesied to have happened.

It is as if something is causing us to split off into a reality alternative to the ones that were predicted. Here is my speculation about the causes for this: that the Sirian intervention in our own evolution together with individual and collective inner work are successfully both allowing us to by-pass the disasters and proceed to the higher dimension in a new and unheard of way: no pole shift, no disasters. Rather, a gradually diminishing of the time-lag between thought and manifestation.

But what happened to the world of the prophecies? Were the prophecies simply wrong? But they have been right in so many ways, and in the case of the Bible Code, as we shall see, spectacularly so. It seems impossible to think that prophetic traditions and instruments that were so accurate should suddenly become mistaken. But the Kogi present another possibility—that we are living in a parallel universe to the one in which the disasters really did happen! The disasters did actually occur—but in another world.

I want to develop this idea a bit so that you can see how it might actually be so.

There was an episode in the original Star Trek series where the Star Ship Enterprise gets caught in some sort of time-energy anomaly. A parallel Enterprise appears in which all the characters—Spock, Captain Kirk, Scotty, and the others—all exist, but they exist as they would have been if their personalities had not grown and matured as Star Fleet officers. All the dark aspects of their individual personalities—anger, egotism, sexual appetite and so forth—become their dominant traits, rather than being, as they are on the "real" Enterprise, momentary aberrations that appear when the otherwise even-tempered and responsible characters are under some strange stress. It is as if there were an alternative parallel universe in which their development had simply not occurred, and they were all there, living their lives in a much less developed state. My speculation is that something like that may be happening at the present time: the cataclysms and disasters—the pole shift, gravitational collapse and the rest—have actually already happened, but because we in fact have been evolving at an unprecedented pace due

to the Sirian intervention in 1972 and to our spiritual efforts—
we have actually shifted into a parallel world where we have
been able to avoid—or temporarily avoid—these terrible
occurrences.

This may sound like a pretty far-fetched way of thinking
about this, but the truth is it is not so different from certain
aspects of the thinking of some present day atomic physicists
and cosmologists.

In modern day quantum physics, there is a theory known
as "the many worlds hypothesis." Quantum physics involves
many interesting paradoxes having to do with the world of
matter smaller than atoms—the world of the so-called elementary particles. Down at that level, reality is not supposed
to be made of discrete bits of matter, but of almost unimag-
inable phenomena that are only clearly expressible in math-
ematical formulae. As I understand it, an elementary particle
is not really a particle or even an ordinary *thing* at all, but
something called a "probability function." Though the idea
is pretty abstract and abstruse, physicists have made various
attempts to explain this reality in more or less ordinary terms.
The only trouble is that when they do so, abandoning clear
mathematics for ordinary language, the results are always
completely paradoxical: you get pictures of worlds, supposed
to be real, that are really quite strange. The "many worlds
hypothesis" is one of these paradoxical attempts to understand the world of elementary particles in ordinary terms. It
goes something like this.

The particular state or condition of a particle—its position in space, how fast it is moving, when it is likely to change
internally—is given by a formula called a "probability function." This formula tells you how *likely* it is—that is, how
probable—that the particle is going to change in a particular way. Here's an analogy from ordinary life. If I wake up
in the morning and see it is raining, there are several possi-

bilities regarding what I might do. Either I won't go outside at all, or if I do I'll take an umbrella, or perhaps I'll forget my umbrella and go out anyway and get wet. These are three different possibilities of what will happen, given that I notice that it is raining. Now different "probabilities" can be assigned to each of these possibilities, regarding which one I am *likely* to take. A "probability" is a numerical value expressing the *degree* of likelihood that some particular thing is going to happen. The probability for each possibility would depend on who I am—whether I am a very busy person and have to go out even though it is raining, or a man of leisure and can afford not to go out at all; whether I am absent-minded and likely to forget my umbrella, or very practical and certain to remember it. So there are three possibilities, and the likelihood of any of them happening depends upon my personal characteristics. The analogy with an elementary particle is that my personal characteristics are like the possible states of the particle, and the likelihood of its changing in various ways would be expressed in the probability function. Now for the elementary particle, this function is all we know about the particle. This is what quantum physics tells us. Physicists like to say that the particle at the bottom *is* its probability function: it *is* the likelihood of its changing in either of its several possible ways.

When an event actually occurs—when the particle does in fact change—the probability function is said to "collapse," i.e., one of the possibilities is realized and the others at that moment seem to be eliminated. Something actually occurs. (I either go outside, or I don't. I either forget my umbrella or I don't.) The other possibilities are now no longer possibilities, so we no longer have a probability function. We have a new fact. But since the physicists think that the reality of the new particle *is* its probability function, this new fact is just a *new* probability function, describing its current state and its new chances of changing into some other condition.

Now the question comes up, since all we know about the particle is its probability of changing—what happened to the possibilities that did *not* occur? Where did they go? Did they just evaporate? Were they unreal to begin with? Well, for the physicists, one way of answering these questions is to assume that in fact they *all* occur, only they occur in parallel universes to the one in which we are making our physical observations! It is as if at the moment that I observed that it was raining outside, three different universes sprang into being: in one of them I decided to stay at home and not go out; in one I went out and took my umbrella, and in a third I went out and, forgetting my umbrella, got soaked. Each of these three universes goes off on its own further journey, entirely separate and out of touch with the others. And in each of these new universes, a new set of possibilities opens up, a new probability function appears, which in turn will "collapse" as a new event occurs, so that the universe is continually splitting apart into new parallel universes every time a decision is made and a set of possibilities becomes a set of parallel realities!

This may sound like a very bizarre universe, but there are many physicists who believe that it truly describes the one in which we really live!

I mention this here only to suggest that it is not so entirely far-fetched to think that the reason we have not experienced the disasters predicted in the prophecies is that we are living in a reality parallel to the one in which they in fact came true. Something very much like this is an important speculation in official, scientifically sanctioned, physical reality!

Transition

Another possibility is that we are living in a kind of transition state between dimensional worlds. Parallel universe or not, most of the conditions that threaten life on Earth make it look like we are very far from being in the fourth dimension (where reality manifests as soon as we think it) or on the third level of consciousness (where we are all spontaneously aware of the unity of all Being). We are still here. Still on the third dimension. And not only that, we inhabit a planet on which the possibility of life itself is threatened. Our abuse of the external technology that we have already invented has polluted our waters and our air, created complicated problems within our ecosystem, crashed holes in the ozone layer, depleted natural resources, and overpopulated the planet to such an extent that nobody knows how long the planet will be able to sustain human life. Our three-dimensional emotional immaturity, self-centeredness, the collective effects of our incompletions from the past, and our limited sense of human possibility, have created enmities between races and nations. Wealth and access to power is increasingly being concentrated in the hands of a small elite, while a larger and larger proportion of the population live in squalor, poverty, and near if not actual slave conditions. From the ordinary perspective of politics and economics, it is a bad joke to think that a world of harmony and Christ Consciousness is just around the corner. Christ Consciousness? Baloney. First we have to clean up the mess we have made for ourselves—if we even survive long enough to be given the chance.

At the same time, think of how complex the world that I have been describing in this book and in my other books really is. It involves many levels of reality: the precession of the equinoxes, the conflict between Michael and Lucifer; the history of the human race with regard to the Sirians and the Nefilim; the solar pulse of 1972 and the holographic protection field; the role of Sacred Geometry; of the five levels of consciousness and the 144 overtones of the octave. It is as though we were becoming aware of a fantastic, multidimensional reality. It is almost as if in following this story out, we are thereby beginning to experience how reality itself has many dimensions, and is occurring simultaneously on many levels or planes. Something is opening up, coming into view, that is very different form the ordinary three-dimensional world that has been the context for world history for the last 13,000 years.

Nevertheless, there is a danger in thinking that our Ascension to the fourth dimension is a matter of course, that everything is "written" once and for all, and that we are in for a free ride to hyper-dimensional glory. In a sense, before we can properly ascend, we will have to descend.

In Order to Ascend We Must Descend

We cannot simply ascend to a fourth-dimensional state without taking care of unfinished business on the third dimension both individually and collectively. Or we can—but to the degree that we do, we will have a very rough time of it, and we will end up taking our unfinished business along with us. This is what happens individually when we pass from one life to another with incomplete intentions and incomplete relationships. And it is what happened to us when we passed from the higher-dimensional reality of Atlantis to where we have been for the past 13,000 years. Or consider the Martians, how they split off from the rest of the Atlanteans and brought a whole series of traumatic and dramatic incompletions with them, including the disaster of the counter-rotating fields in the Bermuda Triangle, and the Secret Government's continuing covert attempts to control the world. So without releasing the suppressed energy and integrating your incompletions, we might ascend, in some sense; but we can't expect that the golden promise of existence without conflict and in a state of perfect harmony with all Being, will be realized, if we ourselves are internally out of whack. In order to truly ascend, we first have to descend—into the bowels of our nature and deal with what we find there. This is not always an easy thing to do.

For many of us, after a lifetime of suppression, so much of our internal body space is taken up with suppressed energy and suppressed memories, that we are almost unable to bear living in our bodies at all. Most people do not actually live in their bodies, for the simple reason that they do not really breathe. They've been holding their breath ever since the first breath of life. But the more you hold your breath the more your body becomes an unpleasant place to be. Unresolved "stuff" just continues to build and to fester; and the more it does, the more you have to withhold awareness from your body, so you hold your breath all the more. It is a vicious circle. If you were living in a house that you hadn't cleaned in twenty years, you probably wouldn't want to spend much time at home! If people haven't cleaned the insides of their bodies, they don't want to spend much time there either.

It is impossible to imagine what ascension and fourth-dimensional reality is really like. But one thing we know for sure is that it involves an intensification of our sense of immediacy—of nowness—of the present. If we are not living in our bodies, we have no access to the present. We evade the present by escaping into fantasies and all sorts of mental constructions. If our bodies are occupied by unconscious formations, we cannot be present in them or present to what is happening in the here and now around us. If we were to be suddenly thrown into a fourth-dimensional state where we had no choice but to be in the present it would be a horribly unpleasant experience. We would run smack up against our resistances. Everything that we have been trying to avoid for our entire life would be forced into the light of day. We would try to contract and suppress all this, and the conflict would become unbearable.

What's true individually is exactly parallel to what is true collectively. It is as if we are all holding our collective breaths as we allow the stench of air pollution and the pollution of our water to accumulate. We try to create artificial environments for ourselves as our natural environment becomes unlivable and the ecosystems necessary to life on Earth whither away. If you think that ascension is just a way of escaping from our own fouled nest—you can forget about it. That's not the way that ascension is going to happen.

For ascension to happen there has to be a massive clean-up operation on two different fronts. We have to clean things up externally and collectively and we have to clean things up individually and internally. The two are actually completely inter-related. The internal clean-up operation is what we have been describing throughout this book: creating an internal environment of safety and trust by declaring that we are already spiritual beings and allowing our incompletions to surface, liberating the energy behind them, and opening to the whole of Being. It is only this that may allow us to pass into a fourth-dimensional state where the problems of pollution simply do not exist. But there has to be an external clean-up too.

The external clean-up operation involves the application of various forms of technology, both internal and external, that in fact are available at the present time. There exists, for instance, a type of special water that was invented by a cer-

tain scientist in Turkey. If you spray this water onto the surface of the most polluted rivers or lakes and allow it to seep
down, it has the power to clear them up. This almost magical stuff actually exists. But for some reason this water is not
being released. It is not being discussed in scientific circles.
There seem to be dark forces in the world today that are preventing it from coming out and being applied. Whether those
forces are the machinations of the Secret Government, or
whether it has to do with there being no way to release it and
make money by doing so, I don't know. I only know that it
is as if the planet itself were not quite ready to recognize
what in fact might be a very simple solution to the entire pollution problem—perhaps because pollution itself corre-
sponds so closely to our own internal state. If we were to
clean up inside and open ourselves to the possibility, there
would be no problem at all in finding a way to clean things
up externally. But it seems that we are not quite ready to do
this, so all sorts of obstacles appear blocking the application
of already existent technologies.

The same thing goes for the so-called energy crisis. An enormous part of the problems we face with the environment comes
from our quest for energy to drive our industries, power our
automobiles and heat our homes. We continue to pollute water
and land with oil spills and other forms of nuclear and chem-
ical contamination that comes from our use of unclean and
unsafe sources of energy, when the possibility for unlimited
amounts of clean "free" energy and the technology to tap it
have been known for almost a century. The story of Nikola
Tesla is an object lesson in where we are in this matter. Tesla
was a Serbian genius who invented alternating current and
dozens of the other technical innovations that were behind the
electronic revolution that ushered in the modern world around
the beginning of the twentieth century. Tesla had discovered
how to tap into the energy of the ether—an unlimited source

of "free," clean energy, that did not require waste-making combustion and could have supplied all of the world with all the energy it needed. The problem was he couldn't get backing to develop his discovery because when J.P. Morgan, the financier behind the growing electric power industry, learned that there was no way to "meter" free energy and turn a profit by distributing it, he blocked Tesla's efforts. Today there is a whole underworld of scientists experimenting with various forms of free energy, solar energy, wind energy, and so forth but they are meeting the same sort of resistance.

So it appears that we have within our grasp the means to clean up the world externally. These means are all examples of left-brain technology. But I strongly suspect that the real secret here is that we have to learn how to apply left-brain technology with the heart chakra open, and that is the key to its becoming available. As long as we approach technology as a means for profit and as something totally impersonal and separate from our inner life we will never be able to solve our problems by these means.

The Indigo Children

Another way that the shift to a higher-dimensional consciousness for the inhabitants of this planet may be occurring is through the apparent mutation of human genetic substance. There are new kinds of human beings appearing on Earth—beings that may very well be the natural bearers of a higher form of consciousness. We are just begin to realize that these children are among us, and nobody knows for sure who they are, why they are here, and what their presence really portends. But Drunvalo and I believe that they may very well be the heralds of the coming shift in dimensional level. Many of their characteristics are just what we would expect if the shift were to come by a basic transmutation of our genetic material.

One group of these new beings are the so-called "Indigo Children." These children were first noticed by a psychically sensitive woman named Nancy Ann Tappe who can perceive the specific spectrum of colors that dominate the human aura.

Nancy Tappe was able to "see" the "life color" of individuals psychically. According to her, there is a basic typology of human auras that indicates, according to dominant color, personality type as well as what the person's mission in life is and what they have come into the world to learn.

She became aware that the spectrum of colors that appear in auras has changed throughout the course of history. She had noticed, for instance, that the personality types associated with the colors fuschia and magenta had disappeared at the beginning of the 20th century. She anticipated that a new personality type would appear towards the end of that century with a new dominant color to replace them. Sometime in the late 1970s she began to notice that children were being born with a dark blue or indigo color as the dominant shade in their auras. Ms. Tappe is not certain when the Indigos actually began to arrive, but she feels that today 90% of all children under ten years old are Indigos, and that before long everyone born will belong to that class.

Since their discovery by Ms. Tappe, psychotherapists have taken note of the Indigos. Lee Carol and John Tober have published a book on them to help parents cope with their charges, since these children really are quite different from other children. The book is called, *The Indigo Children: The New Kids Have Arrived.* The authors list ten characteristics that distinguish the Indigos, all of which indicate that these people come into the world with a much more vivid sense of who they are as spiritual beings than other people, suggesting that they may already be living, at least in part, on a fourth dimensional level.

Being an Indigo is not without its downside, however, and

though they may in fact be here to lead the way to a new level of consciousness for the entire planet, if they are not understood and treated appropriately, their extraordinary abilities may help to bring about disasters rather than to save us from them.

Here are the ten characteristics that the authors mention (this is my paraphrase):

1. A feeling of "royalty": They seem to know without being told that they are spiritual beings, and they tend to carry themselves with a certain sense of dignity and certainty about who they are.

2. They know that they deserve to be here and are surprised when they find that older people don't necessarily feel that way. They simply do not understand the ideas of "low self-esteem," guilt, or a sense of inferiority or subservience. It is as if they simply are not afflicted with "victim-consciousness" at all—at least if they are appreciated and allowed to develop in their own way.

3. They do not need to be told who they are, or educated or trained to have a feeling of self-respect. Sometimes they give startling and disconcerting accounts of their own nature.

4. They do have a problem with any form of authority imposed upon them. It is not that they are disrespectful or fundamentally rebellious. It is just that they do not understand authority that is exerted without explanation and without their consent's being requested.

5. There are things they simply will not do. They will not wait in lines for example! They will not waste time just for the sake of obeying a rule to keep them in order.

6. Generally they are irritated by imposed order and rules of behavior or organization that do not encourage or allow them to use their own creativity to deal with the situation.

7. They are extremely creative socially. They find spontaneous and positive ways of interacting with each other, and they can see through ordinary ways of doing things, both at home and at school. They tend to be disinclined to obey the rules when they see ways of improving upon them. This makes them seem to be nonconformists and rebellious, but their basic motive is to make things work more smoothly and for the good of all.

8. They prefer to be with other Indigos or other people on their level of consciousness, and can appear unfriendly and even anti-social when others of their kind are not around. They can become morose and inward and quite sensitive to being misunderstood. This can cause real problems at school where they frequently are misperceived as learning-disabled or hyperactive. These misdiagnoses are quite dangerous.

9. It is impossible to make them "behave" by guilt-tripping them or threatening them with disapproval. They know who they are in a way that lower-dimensional beings can hardly conceive of, and cannot be made to feel that they are inferior beings. When threatened, they in fact can become quite violent. Nancy Tappe believes that the children who have over the last decade or so been involved in acts of violence against teachers, parents, or peers, have in every case been Indigo children.

10. They are not shy. They know what they need and generally have no difficulty in making you aware of it.

Part IV

The
Bible Code

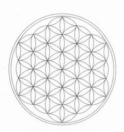

The Bible Code and Destiny

I want to include as the concluding section of this book an account of the "Bible Code."

In recent years there has been a lot of excitement about discoveries made by Israeli and other scholars that the Hebrew text of the Torah, the Five Books of Moses, is actually a complex code, containing prophecies and other information about history and possibly about the future. Two important books on the subject—*The Bible Code* by Michael Drosnin, and *Cracking the Bible Code* by Jeffrey Satinover, have become best sellers. They tell the story of how the code was discovered and contain detailed speculations on its significance and scope. According to Drunvalo Melchizedek, however, the information contained in the Bible Code actually far exceeds the researches of these scholars—it contains in detail the entire Akashic Record from the time of the rise of Atlantis until some time in the 28th century A.D. But though this record is quite complete it still has built into it certain points where change is possible, i.e, there are degrees of freedom available to us. Everything is not completely decided. The code itself is constructed so that depending on how deeply we have penetrated its secrets, different pictures of our future are embedded in it. In that way the code is like reality itself: what it contains is a function of our consciousness of it.

The following is an account what is really behind the writing of the Bible and the complex and wonderful code that is its reason for being.

The Hebrews

When the 1,000 Ascended Masters who had been trained on Lemuria arrived on one of the ten islands of the newly arisen Atlantis—the island of Undal—they structured the island like a living brain: they built a wall from north to south, forty feet high and twenty feet wide, and they built a smaller wall from east to west, so the island was divided into four quadrants. The two quadrants on the left corresponded to the left "male" hemisphere of the brain; the two on the right to the right "female" hemisphere. They divided themselves into groups, 500 on each side. Then they projected onto the main island of Atlantis the form of the Tree of Life *(figure 4.1)*—one of the forms that can be taken from the Flower of Life—the pattern from which all individual forms in the universe derive.

The Tree of Life pattern may be familiar to many readers from the Hebrew Kabbala and from the Kabbalistic tradition that is part of Western esotericism. What the connection between this form and the Hebrew people really is will become clear as we go on.

The Tree of Life is a figure consisting of ten spheres arranged in the pattern given in *figure 4.1*. Each of the spheres is really a whirling vortex of energy and represents one of the ten basic energy types available for conscious beings. Each of us belongs to one of these energy types. Being strongly attracted to or repelled by other beings or by places or situations has a lot to do with how our particular energy vortex resonates with them. On the Tree of Life the ten vortices are balanced in a particular way, and the relationship between the vortices spells out all the possibilities for interaction between different kinds of living beings.

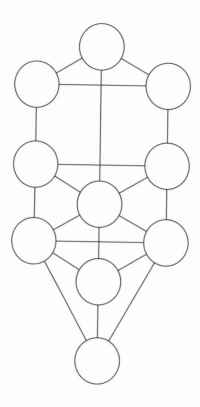

Figure 4–1. The Tree of Life.

When the Tree of Life was set up on the main island of Atlantis, the vortices were set in motion and they sent out powerful subliminal waves toward the Lemurians, who were now inspired by an urge to migrate to Atlantis. Lemuria had already fully sunk into the sea by this time. The Lemurians were a highly developed right-brain culture—they were highly developed intuitively—so they had been aware that the end was coming and had migrated to the west coast of the Americas. At the point we are talking about they already occupied the land from as far south as Lake Titicaca to as far north as Mt. Shasta. Now the energy frequencies of the vortices coming from Undal resonated with Lemurians of the corresponding energetic type. The population of Lemuria, however, only contained eight out of the ten possible types, and so after the great migration to Atlantis, there were two vortices that had not drawn any living beings to them.

It is important to understand that the energy waves going out from the Tree of Life did not only emanate in three-dimensional space. They flowed both forward and backward in *time,* and they captured the notice of two species of extra-terrestrial beings, one from deep in the past and one from far in the future. The species from the past were the ancient Martians. The species from the future were the Hebrews. (These Hebrews, by the way, are both the ancestors and the descendents of the present day Jewish people, though the Jewish people are not aware of the process that they are undergoing.)

This is how it happened that there were both Martians and Hebrews on the continent of Atlantis.

The Martians came from far in the past indeed—almost one million years in fact. And in order to escape an already profoundly compromised environment, the Martians built an "external Merkaba" and migrated to Atlantis—that is, to about 900,000 years in their future, or 65,000 years ago in *our* past. The story of how the Hebrews happened to travel there is, according to Drunvalo, as follows.

Drunvalo doesn't know where the Hebrews originally came from. But he says they were extremely highly evolved beings living in the twenty-eighth century, and that some-how, in a way that we are not able to understand, they made an enormous collective spiritual blunder. The consequences of this blunder were that they created conditions for them-selves that were incredibly unpleasant. Since beings on the fourth dimension and beyond unerringly create the condi-tions of their lives instantaneously with their thought, and since the Hebrews were highly evolved beings, we can only imagine that their blunder was in their way of thinking. But what it was we do not know.

In any event, what happened to them, Drunvalo says, was that they were forced to repeat a part of their evolutionary process. It is as if they were school children that got "left back" and had to repeat, say, the fourth grade in elementary school. Only for them repeating the grade meant going back in time about 65,800 years—to Atlantis, to the second of the two empty vortices, to attempt to reprogram their being and to undo the error that caused such unimaginably horrid conditions to manifest about them.

Now in Atlantis, right up until its destruction, all human beings existed on the first level of consciousness and therefore, since everyone had access to Dream Time memory, there was no need to develop writing to keep track of what happened. But the Hebrews, who arrived at Atlantis from the twenty-eighth century, knew that a time was coming when the human race would lose access to this kind of memory. Yet in order to complete their task, they needed to have access to their own past (which was also, from their point of view, their future! I will explain this in a moment.) In any case, by some means—and we do not know precisely how— either because they "remembered" some form of writing they had known in their time in the twenty-eighth century, or by some other form of memory far more sophisticated than either Dream Time or writing, they proceeded to write down the entire Akashic Record from their own time in Atlantis up until the twenty-eighth century.

The introduction of writing itself, by the way, was undertaken by Thoth personally in the early dynasties of Egypt. And the reason he did this was that he knew that writing would *destroy* the Dream Time memory and throw humanity from the first level onto the second. Though this seems to involve an immense loss—the loss of fourth dimensional consciousness and the awareness of the Unity of Being—it was absolutely necessary. It was necessary because the Ascended Masters' solution to the problem that had been created in Atlantis was to accelerate the development of human consciousness. If they could get us from the first to the third level —to a higher form of Unity Consciousness—that would solve the problem. But in order to do that we would have to be brought through the stepping stone of the second level.

Drunvalo's angels told him that the Hebrews had to repeat their own evolutionary process in order to correct the errors they had made that had resulted in incredibly horrible conditions for them. The angels said that the Hebrews would be able to do this by making essential changes in certain central places in history, and only in those central places. But before they came back to the past to repeat their evolution, they needed to have a map of history so they could locate those precise points that had to be changed. For this reason they had to retain in some way the Akashic Record. The Akashic Record is something like a perfect cosmic memory. It is the trace of everything that ever happened, everything that was ever thought or felt or imagined by anyone anywhere. The Hebrews were able to record the Akashic Record in absolute detail up to the moment that they recorded it, that is up to their time in the twenty-eighth century. And they brought that record back with them to Atlantis. How did they record it and transport it? We don't know. We only know that by the time the Torah was written down—around the tenth century B.C.—it contained encoded in it the entire of the Hebrews' knowledge of the Akashic Record.

Obviously, writing as we know it could not possibly record all the information contained in the Akashic Record. What was required was a way of containing a staggeringly huge amount of information in a relatively short text. In other words, they had to invent a very powerful system for encoding information. Today we understand very well that this is possible from our computers and their microchips, which are able similarly to hold tremendous amounts of data in tiny spaces. What the Hebrews produced was the five volumes that are known as the Torah, the first five books of the Bible, familiar to modern Jewish people and revered as The Five Books of Moses. The rabbis of all periods have thought of the Torah as an extraordinary book, created by Almighty God and delivered by Moses to the Children of Israel on Mt. Sinai while they were wandering in the desert after having escaped from Egypt.

After the fall of Atlantis, the Hebrews, like everyone else who survived, no longer existed on the fourth dimensional level, and so no longer knew exactly what this text that they had created really was. Its very existence was kept as a deep secret for the entire length of time between the fall of Atlantis and the time the Hebrews came together and formed the nation of ancient Israel, about three thousand years ago. At that time the Torah itself was revealed, but only the most superficial aspect of it was remembered and taught to the people—the stories and laws that are contained at the literal level of the text.

The leaders of the Hebrews, the learned rabbis whose whole life was devoted to studying the Torah, actually did retain an inkling that the stories and laws were not all that there was to it. They knew that there were secrets buried within the script of the Torah, and they used various means to decipher these messages. In fact, as we shall see, the ultimate decoding of the Torah—the discovery that has been made over the last ten years and referred to popularly as "The Bible Code"—was accomplished first by Orthodox Jewish scholars who had been studying the Torah in these traditional ways.

The Torah as Code in Jewish Tradition

A special feature of written Hebrew that makes it particularly good for containing multiple meanings and expressing a code is the fact that ordinarily no vowel sounds are written down. Written Hebrew is a little like the form of shorthand known as "speed writing"—the phrase "he revealed a book" might look like "h rvld bk." Now, according to the rabbis, the Torah can also be written with the spaces between the words left out, for example, "hrvldbk." When this is done the long chain of letters becomes a code and the letters can be redivided in new ways. Instead of "he revealed a book" we might have "hr vld bk" which could mean "her veiled book."

Another feature of the Hebrew language that made it good for holding multiple meanings and encoding information is the fact that each Hebrew letter is also a numeral—a number. When a reader of Hebrew sees a string of letters he also sees a string of numbers. The rabbis said that when the numbers represented by the letters of a certain word add up to a certain number, any other word whose numbers add up to the same number must have a special relation to the original word. For example the Hebrew words for Unity and for Love added up to the same numerical value.

The rabbis possess many traditions for understanding the additional meanings contained in the Torah when looked at this way. These traditions are part of the mystical aspect of Jewish teachings—the Kabbala. Many rabbis spent their whole lives studying the Torah searching for these meanings. In fact, in present day Israel and in Jewish communities in other parts of the world there are rabbis who still do.

Now, when a coded message is transmitted, it is very important that every symbol of the code be copied exactly and that there be no mistakes in the transcription. A single error might make the message completely unintelligible. Accordingly, extraordinary care must be taken to make sure that no errors creep into it. The Jewish tradition has always treated the Torah with just this kind of meticulous care. Copies of the Torah can only be made by hand, on special kinds of parchment, and written on scrolls, not leaves of paper. Specially trained "scribes" who dedicate their lives to the art of copying the Torah are the only persons who engage in this work. If the scribe makes a single error while copying a scroll, the whole scroll must be destroyed. No smudging. No erasing. The result of this extraordinary care has been that the ancient text of the Torah has been transmitted over time with great accuracy. In the written record of other ancient peoples—the Romans or the Greeks, for instance—there are usually many variant versions of any given text, variations that have been caused by errors in copying over the centuries. Not so with the Torah. Scrolls discovered near the Dead Sea in the 1940s and written during the first century of the common era are identical to copies of the Torah that we have from the Middle Ages and from more recent times.

How the Bible Code Works

Treating the Torah as a code has always been part of the Jewish tradition, as I mentioned, and this made it possible for rabbis to find many profound and hidden meanings under the surface of the text of the Bible. But when Drunvalo speaks of the Bible Code he is not speaking of this tradition, but of very recent discoveries made by several Israeli scholars using modern code-breaking techniques and checking their discoveries with sophisticated methods of statistical analysis. These new messages and this new kind of code-breaking was first discovered by a rabbi who was working in the traditional way, as I also mentioned before, so there is a connection between the Jewish tradition and the cracking of the Bible Code. But the Bible Code was broken using "decryption" (code-breaking) methods invented by the Allies during World War II in their effort to crack the military codes used by the Nazis.

The way the code works is fascinating and I will give you a taste of it. But first I should tell you what kind of messages can be found in it and how scholars discovered that these new kinds of messages were there. First of all there is a tradition going back to a saying of a famous rabbi of the Middle Ages known as the Gaon of Vilna. This rabbi has a statement that the Torah contains absolutely everything about creation in it. It was believed that the Torah was not only the *story* of the creation of the world and the story of world history, but that it contains the very pattern *by which* the world was created and the very template for history itself. In other worlds, looking at the Torah, we are looking at the very mind of God. It was not that the rabbis thought they understood the Torah in full detail. It was simply that based on this belief, the activity of studying the Torah took on an immense significance, for in devoting oneself to its study and interpretation, one was directly participating in God's thoughts. So the study and interpretation of the Torah, apart from living by its teachings and obeying its laws, was in itself a kind of mystical worship.

What we will see is that according to Drunvalo, the Torah does indeed contain "everything," but in a way that the Hebrews themselves had forgotten.

Now another way that the rabbis had of discovering coded meanings in the Torah was to find words in the string of letters by skipping over equal numbers of letters and reading the words that were formed by the letters selected when the skipped letters were ignored. For instance, look at the string of English letters:

… cegyptsdhshggdhhermesdpjsgodsqajosstl

tpjggpsklmxhppuspmngss …

If we start with the first time the letter "t" appears and skip the next ten letters, read the letter we land on, skip ten again, and so forth, we find the name "Thoth" spelled out:

… cegyp$T$sdhshggpdh$H$ermesdpjsg$O$dsqajosstl

Tpjggpsklmx$H$ppuspmngss …

By continuing in this way, one might find all kinds of hidden messages by simply choosing the right number of letters to skip and knowing where to stop and start. This in itself might be intriguing but not very startling. But what the code-breakers discovered was that if you laid out the text of the Torah in a grid so that the letters selected by skipping lined up one above the other in columns, other words in rows crossing the selected letters would appear that were significantly related to the chosen word. The grid for the above message would look like this:

… cegyp$T$sdhsh

ggpdh$H$ermes

dpjsg$O$dsqaj

osstl$T$pjggp

sklmx$H$ppuspmngss …

Now, if you look at the letters that either cross or lie next to the letters T H and O of the name Thoth, you find the words "Egypt," "Hermes," and "God":

... cegyp**T**sdhsh

ggpdh**Hermes**

dpjs**g****O****d**sqaj

osstl**T**pjggp

sklmx**H**ppuspmngss ...

Of course these words appear in these places because I have
constructed the string of letters on purpose so that when
decoded by the proper method—namely knowing where to
begin and skipping every ten letters and then writing out the
letters in a grid in this fashion—the message would appear. It
would be very strange indeed if you found such a message in
a text which had not been constructed in this way. But I am
jumping ahead.

What earlier Hebrew scholars knew was that the names
of certain Biblical prophets and other important personages
were hidden in passages of the Torah by the encoding pro-
cedure I just described. And they developed a method for
searching for these "encrypted" or encoded names. Finding
the name depended upon first finding the right number of
letters to skip between the letters. Searching for the encoded
name was then a matter of trying out different intervals—
different amounts of letters of to skip—until the name appeared. You could try all the intervals beginning with one
(skipping one letter), then trying two letters, all the way up
to the total number of letters in the Torah. Also you could
begin with the first time the first letter of the prophet's name
appears in the Torah, then begin with the second time that
same letter appeared, and so on. This would give you many
chances of finding the name you are looking for, and there-

fore it would not be unlikely, if you had enough time and patience, that you would find it. The role that computers played in cracking the Bible Code was that it became possible to use them to conduct these searches very rapidly and to conduct many searches at the same time.

You can see, as I mentioned, that it is very likely that if you searched the entire Torah using all the possible intervals and starting at all the occurrences of the first letters of the name, that you would find the right name. But what is not so likely is that you would find words or phrases closely related to the chosen name crossing it or in parts of the grid in its immediate neighborhood. But that is just what the scholars found.

It was this that got the scholars excited. For it seemed that it was incredibly unlikely for these neighboring messages just to be in there by chance, and if not by chance, how could they have gotten in there except by being put there? But the truly amazing part of the story is yet to come.

Not satisfied with the names of characters in the Torah, the scholars initiated searches for the names of important people in Jewish religious history—mostly famous rabbis and authors—from periods long after the Torah was written—and guess what: they were in there too! And not only that, but relevant information about them was found crossing their names.

Next the scholars searched for names of persons significant to the Jewish people or the State of Israel for other than religious reasons. They looked up Adolf Eichmann, for instance, and found his name crossed by, "He consumed a great people in Auschwitz." They looked up Anwar Sadat, the Egyptian leader who made an accord with Israel and was assassinated on October 6, 1981 for it. In Sadat's case the words in the vicinity of his name gave the date, the setting, and even the name of the assassin himself. All this meant that not only were there names of future persons mentioned in the Torah, but future historical events were known by the Torah too. The Torah had future history encoded inside it. How could this be? For it seemed to imply that the author of the Torah had known in advance the names and circumstances of important interpreters of the Torah generations before they were born, and knew events in the history of the Jewish people literally thousands of years before they occurred. Who but God could know such things? The Bible Code seemed to confirm the Divine authorship of the Torah.

Now you can imagine the excitement this caused for people who believe in the Jewish or the Christian religions. But you can also imagine the consternation and commotion it caused among people who don't—atheists and others who are committed to the idea that the Bible is nothing but a compilation of *human* writings. The consequence was an intensive effort to find the flaw in the scholars' methods and reasoning—to show that the findings, in spite of appearances, were really due to chance.

The science for determining whether something is due to chance or is part of some intentional pattern is called the "theory of probability." It is commonly used to calculate the "odds" on horse races or dice tables, and the actuarial tables that insurance companies use to calculate premiums. The statisticians and experts in the theory of probability became very interested in trying to find out if these hidden messages were genuinely as improbable as they seemed. Encryption experts from Hebrew University at Jerusalem, Harvard University, as well as the U.S. government at the Pentagon were brought in. They subjected the code to the most rigorous analyses imaginable.

It was particularly difficult to perform the appropriate analysis of the code, because it was very difficult to define quite exactly what the messages were probabilities *of.* For instance, if a single die has six faces, each inscribed with a numeral from 1 to 6, and if the die is not loaded or otherwise improperly "skewed," the chances are exactly 1 in 6, on any given throw, that any particular number will turn up. But what corresponded to the six faces in the Bible Code? How could you calculate the odds that the Torah would or would not contain the messages they apparently contained? This is what challenged the statisticians. They found that you can indeed do it, but that the calculation is extremely complex. To date the results are still controversial, though by and large the analyses have shown that at least some of the results are as enormously improbable as they seem intuitively; And for the results that are definitively known to be positive—that is, not the product of chance—they are staggeringly positive. In other words, the Bible Code is real. So the question that began the search—if not by chance by whom or what?—remains.

The Bible Code now really does seem to contain hidden messages about people and events connected with Jewish history and with periods long after the Torah itself was written. It would seem that this meant not only that God really did write the Torah, but that history itself was something that is predetermined and fixed. Did this mean that a kind of absolute Fate rules events? That things are already settled as to how they are going to turn out, and that there is nothing we or anyone can do about them? With this in mind, the Bible scholars began to devise questions to test the Bible Code to see just how much is contained in it. It would seem that if the code contained information about the future and we can correctly interpret that information, we might be able to take steps to avoid the predicted outcome and thus prove the prediction wrong!

You can see how important this question is. We have become aware—apart from the Bible Code—how perilous our circumstances are at this time on Earth—dangers threaten the very existence of life on the planet. And we surely want to know whether it is absolutely fated that these dangers will end in complete disaster for us, or if there is some kind of way out, and even more importantly, what that way out is. Well, scholars have found that almost every time they tested the code it has proved correct, but that a startling feature has emerged in the code that showed that whatever being composed it was not an absolute "fatalist" at all. Here is the story of how.

Open Destiny

There are a small number of particular historical events that the Bible Code seemed to predict were going to happen that in fact did not happen. For instance, there was a prediction that Jerusalem was going to be destroyed by a nuclear explosion. The exact circumstances were specified. The exact date and time were given, but when that time rolled around, nothing happened. In nearly every other instance where the Bible Code predicted a specific event, it had occurred. But here it seemed to have failed. What does this mean?

Well let's look again at our picture of the grid in which the Bible Code reveals its meanings. We saw that extraordinary messages appeared that crossing the vertical column of letters that spelled out the name under investigation. But among the other letters in the vicinity of the name there were sometimes found other words and phrases that were significant too. For the grid surrounding the name of Anwar Sadat, for instance, the name of his assailant was found not far away, as I mentioned before. Now what scholars found in regard to the bombing of Jerusalem was that if they "expanded the matrix," additional messages pertinent to the question appeared. By "expanding the matrix" I mean looking at a larger area around the selected name so that more combinations of letters could appear, and other messages could be found, if they were there. What scholars found in the case of the bombing of Jerusalem that didn't happen was the word "delayed," and a little further away the question, "Will you change this?" Apparently the code itself was not fatalistic at all but included specific messages regarding just where things could be changed and its own predictions avoided. Just like the prophecies of Nostradamus or Edgar Cayce, at least some of the prophecies in the Bible Code are indeed put there in the hopes that they would turn out to be wrong!

This possibility of avoiding "fated" outcomes is truly what is most important about the bible Code, for it promises that there are specific ways in which apparently inevitable disasters can be "delayed." And if we "change this," i.e., make the necessary changes in our way of thinking, in our specific thoughts, and in the way we conduct our inner lives, they can be completely avoided or transformed.

Drunvalo tells us of two other instances in very recent times when we in fact did manage to avoid disasters of a magnitude even greater than the detonation of a nuclear device over Jerusalem. I want to the tell the story of these instances, because it illustrates something very beautiful about the actual way these changes can happen. For the sake of the logic of the story I'm going to give the third and most recent "wrong" prediction first. That prediction had to do with the disturbances in Kosovo in the spring of 1999. The prediction was that on April 8, events in Kosovo would start off a chain of other events that would lead to World War III.

According to what the angels told Drunvalo, there were elements in Yugoslavia that were secretly connected with Saddam Hussein; and the reason that the trouble in Kosovo came to a head at that time was that these elements wanted to implicate the entire Moslem world to the point where Jihad

would be declared. Jihad, you may be aware, means the declaration of an ultimate "Holy War" between the followers
of Mohammed and all other peoples. Jihad can only be
declared when all the Moslem countries are unanimous that
the time is right. Saddam Hussein wished, and as far as we
know still wishes, to unite the Moslem world in a war against
the West, and the only way to do that is by inciting the declaration of Jihad. The actual aim of the Gulf War in 1991,
from Saddam Hussein's point of view, was to initiate that
"Holy War."

You may remember that after the allies had chased the
Iraqis out of Kuwait, they began an invasion of Iraq, but that
the invasion was suddenly aborted before Hussein himself
could be killed or captured or the Iraqi arsenals destroyed.
At the time it was very hard to understand why President
Bush had ordered the end of the invasion before he completed it. The reason was that the allies' intelligence learned
that Hussein had deposited large quantities of anthrax in
Jerusalem, and that if the invasion of Iraq had continued, the
anthrax would have been released. This in fact was the second prediction—that anthrax would be released in Jerusalem.

After the Gulf War Saddam Hussein succeeded in spread-
ing secret stashes of anthrax throughout the Western world.
The anthrax is ready to be released on a moment's notice—
just a phone call from Saddam Hussein and Jihad would
begin in that form. But again, Jihad cannot be declared without the unanimity of the Moslem world. The third prediction was that events in Kosovo would create that unanimity
and World War III would begin.

Drunvalo was in Germany conducting a workshop just
before the "doomsday" date of April 8 arrived, and he was
told by his angels that this workshop was going to be the
most important workshop he had ever given. He was told of
the events about to happen in Kosovo, and that the work-

shop would determine whether these events would lead to Jihad and to the beginning of the war, or whether humanity, through Drunvalo and the members of the workshop, would be able "to change this."

Now there is a belief among many Germans that, just as they had caused World War II, they would eventually be able to atone for it by preventing World War III. There were about one-hundred people in the workshop. Drunvalo explained to them the seriousness of what they had to do, and they understood. This created an incredibly powerful context for their work, as you can imagine. They sat down in meditation together, and for two hours these one-hundred people melded their entire beings into one being, with one intent. It was if they had passed into the center of the Earth as a single mind. Then they emerged. The events in Kosovo happened. But no Jihad.

There are two important messages in this story. The first is how the creation of a context can motivate and empower our internal practices. The second is that the way we can change the future is by developing our inner being individually and collectively. It is internal work and only internal work that can bring us into a parallel reality and allow us to by-pass disasters that would otherwise be inevitable.

The Future of the Possible

Now this question of "changing history" is precisely what the Hebrews in the twenty-eighth century—should we say "were" or "will be" faced with? They had created an intolerable reality, and they were traveling backwards in time to try to change it. This is an interesting example of how little we know about the workings of "destiny" or "karma" and "history." It seems impossible to think about how it might be possible for events in the future to influence events in the past. But the lesson that history itself can be changed is something we need to take extremely seriously. (Incidentally, today there are physicists who are working to understand the possibility of time travel on the basis of what they call "back action"—a phenomenon known to occur among sub-atomic particles that amounts to the future turning around and causing something to happen in the past.)

The reason that we must take these strange ideas and possibilities seriously has to do with what it means concretely to have access to higher-dimensional realities. In *Nothing* I told the stories of the Philadelphia and the Montauk experiments. These two experiments were linked in a kind of hyper-time: one took place on August 12, 1943, and one took place on August 12, 1983, but actually they were part of the same hyper-dimensional event. One could imagine a higher-dimensional perspective sending out rays of action into our historical time. Beings on a higher dimension would be able to act "simultaneously" at many different moments "here," while all the "while" "developing" in their own dimension, in their own time, in a way we cannot imagine.

When we become aware of the Merkaba field surrounding our bodies and realize that that field itself exists on a higher dimension, we begin to understand that we ourselves *already exist* higher dimensionally. For instance, it is already completely true at this moment, that each one of us *has* a Merkaba field that exists as our true nature. This fact is, relative to our own personal history as we know it, something that we will come to know in the future. But it is true "timelessly." We are what we are ultimately for all eternity. We only come to know it as we evolve in time. But for us, our Merkaba field is something in the future. Yet we can begin to come to have an experience of it now by practicing the meditation given in *Nothing*. The way we experience our lives changes dramatically as we begin to experience our Merkaba field.

For us, our Higher Self, Unity or Christ Consciousness exists in the realm of Possibility. Possibility is the realm of the future; but when we declare that reality itself is essentially the realm of the Possible, we know that the future is Now.

For information regarding Rebirthing and Flower of Life workshops, and to receive a list of available books, tapes, and videos, write to:

Bob Frissell
c/o North Atlantic Books
P.O. Box 12327
Berkeley CA 94712

Website: www.bobfrissell.com

Please include a self-addressed stamped envelope.